ZEN
AND THE
LAST HURRAH

In the wheel-tracks of **Robert Pirsig**
across back country America

Des Molloy

Kahuku
Publishing Collective

Publishing Collective

Zen and The Last Hurrah
In the wheel-tracks of Robert Pirsig across
back country America

© **Des Molloy 2021**

Text design by The Design Dept.
Cover design by The Design Dept.
www.thedesigndept.com.au
Display font: Scribbling Tom by Tom Chalky
Body font: Cronos Pro

Editing by Mary Bennett at
www.proofreading.co.nz

Photo Acknowledgement: Robert M. Prisig
1968, backcover, pp. 155. All other images
belong to Des Molloy.

Excerpts from *Zen and the Art of Motorcycle
Maintenance* by Robert M. Pirsig. Copyright
(c) 1974 by Robert M. Pirsig. Used by
permission of HarperCollins Publishers.

Acknowledgement: Professor Henry S Gurr's
stewardship of all things relating to *Zen and
the Art of Motorcycle Maintenance*.
http://venturearete.org/ResearchProjects/
ProfessorGurr/Main/HomePage

Printed and bound in USA
by Cushing-Malloy, Inc.

Published in 2021 by
Kahuku Publishing
PO Box 149 Takaka
Tasman 7142, New Zealand
www.kahukupublishing.com

ISBN. PB: 978-0-473-54777-6
      ePub: 978-0-473-54778-3
      Kindle: 978-0-473-54779-0

I have been lucky in life to have my wonderful wife Stephanie behind me, sometimes as a pillion but always as a support … a buttress against criticism. She waves me goodbye stoically and welcomes me home enthusiastically. Long may it continue.

ZEN AND THE LAST HURRAH

IV

CONTENTS

ZEN AND THE LAST HURRAH

Chapter 1

GESTATION

It was a dark and stormy night ... well actually it wasn't, but that is such a great start to a story. I could fib and transfer my epiphany back a couple of days, when it really was stormy, but I'm not sure I could live with that. The true night in question was Sunday 4th February 2006 at about 10 pm, and as there is just the slightest possibility that somebody out there among you is a stickler for accuracy and who has an amazing memory or access to New Zealand's NIWA (National Institute of Water and Atmospheric Research) records for that night, I'd better stick to the facts, otherwise I'd be pointed out as a fraud – a pathetic attention-seeking fraud. So I'll start as I mean to go on, by telling the truth. It was dark and it was night ... it just wasn't stormy. So that sets the scene for the beginning of this saga. I know exactly how it all started ... where the tiny embryo that began as a day-dream (actually a night-dream) came from. I was just finishing a mini-adventure ... so now I have to back up a bit and tell you a little about that mini-adventure so I can reveal the magic moment that gives this tale the title and its substance.

I'd ridden my dear old 1937 BSA Empire Star, known to all as Bessie, up to New Zealand's annual classic motorcycle racing festival at Pukekohe, near Auckland. In the parlance of the young, it had been a *mish* ... a real mission! The adventure was also part of a landmark challenge that I had put together for my motorcycling friends and club mates. I had called it the Wanderers And Nomads, Know Every Road challenge, to give it an interesting acronym, and I listed 32 interesting places around New Zealand, giving them all points, and the aim was to get as many points as you could in a year. I had indicated that there would be a trophy and I had introduced a handicap so if the bike was older or a pillion was being carried etc., got you more points. The races at Pukekohe got a big score, and by detouring up the tortuous gravel road along the Whanganui River, we'd aimed to get some good points at Pipiriki on Friday night, go to Pukekohe on Saturday and pick up a few more from having a beer at the historic DeBretts Hotel in Taupō on the way home. Excellent plan!

The Friday ride had corresponded with some of the heaviest rain that I could remember being out in on two wheels. Not only was it wet, but Bessie was ailing for some reason, intermittently stuttering and seeming to overheat on occasion, almost to the point of seizing. What a night to be camping out. Fortunately and coincidentally, along the way, we had encountered Robert who had the keys to a workmate's holiday home near Lake Taupo, so when Pipiriki was too wet, we carried on through the night, a wonderfully mismatched trio of bikes and riders sharing the adversity with the camaraderie that comes easily to motorcyclists. There was tall, silvered, elegant and erudite Winton on his magnificent Ducati Multistrada, a bike that looks like it could be ridden anywhere (even the name proclaims it as 'many roads' with the advertising puffery, "any road, any time") … until you show it gravel or some wet clay. The blood-red pride of Italy gained some scars that night when both were encountered. Jovial, affable, sturdy, swarthy Robert the lawyer was on the rare and beautiful, Phillipe-Starke-styled, orange and silver, quirky Aprilia Moto 6.5, the twin of one that had been stolen from us a couple of months earlier. And there was me – say no more Des, you promised to tell the truth.

The Friday had ended after midnight with all of us knackered and soaked to the skin. Everything we had on was sodden, each of us embarrassed at not being as weathertight as we should have been. I think we had all become blasé over the years and also now sometimes motorcyclists' gear is more about marketing and pose than function – lots of armour and breathability and gussets, expensive as hell, pockets for Africa, but nowhere near the waterproofing of an industrial plastic coat. A late-night/early-morning meal was cobbled up from some dehydrated food I had with me, clothes were hung all over the garage and a warm, cosy night was had. The morning brought the realisation that our clothes were still wet and we laughed at our stupidity. In our befuddled fatigued state we hadn't even put everything in the hot-water cupboard ... just the cell phones. I desperately and ineffectually tried ironing my denim shirt dry on the floor but got a bit shy when the others took photos of me. So it would have to be body warmth to do the moisture removal. Our gonads might shrivel up and wither away during that slow process, but we all knew that we'd get through it, and just as night follows day, so does warm and dry follow wet and cold ... sooner or later.

All this is just setting the scene, so I won't linger on the delights of seeing and hearing 350 classic racing motorbikes or wandering, nothing like lonely-as-a-cloud, among thousands of race enthusiasts' interesting bikes. This is the one weekend where we all show off our goodies, be it a BSA Bantam, Norton International, Brough Superior, an SFC Laverda or a pre-war Indian Scout. With two-wheels in the garage at home, you'd no more take the Toyota Corolla to this race meet than wear Speedos to work on a hot day. They might be suitable but so inappropriate. Sadly, there is only so long you can stay at these events meeting up with old friends, making new ones etc. Robert and Winton both had other things to do on Sunday so headed off early at different times. I think each was relishing the opportunity to give their modern steeds their heads and let them stretch their legs in the way that you can't help doing after you've watched motor racing. Before leaving, Robert had posed the Aprilia appearing to enter a Portaloo. I forget the caption from the resulting photo, so it can't really have been all that memorable, although I thought so at the time.

Finally, on Sunday afternoon, I had to 'face the fear and do it anyway'. Being 600 km away from home on a 69-year-old motorbike, faced with half of the ride having to be after dark and with no back-up by way of support vehicle, can be a bit daunting if you let it seem a big deal. The secret is to not worry about things that might not happen. Despite being known by all as the 'Prince of Darkness', Joe Lucas's 6-volt lighting might not dim, the engine might not seize, you mightn't get a puncture, the old cork-lined clutch mightn't slip and the magneto mightn't fail. Quite a few mightn'ts, but every turn of the wheel is a turn closer to home. The little fears that this sort of ride introduces are trifles that shouldn't ever mean that you stay at home and don't do it … or almost as bad, if you put the bike on a trailer and tow it behind the 'pleased-and-proud' family saloon. The reward of the incredulous "you rode where? … on that old thing?" is always worth the effort and discomfort.

As I have grown older, I have grown … not wiser or richer … just grown. This has meant that the svelte little BSA that was such a nice bike to flick around the twisties in the 1970s is quite a cramped squeeze 30 years later. This makes a long ride an endurance test. Any long ride on a motorbike needs resilience, and a long ride on a pre-war, rigid-rear-ended, girder-forked old fossil that is really too small for you just needs more resilience. Long rides allow and encourage personal reflection. There is a hell of a long time with no one to talk to but the bike. I know sometimes we sing, but despite riding for over 40 years in over 40 countries and singing on many a long ride, I still don't know the words to many songs. In the words of Steppenwolf, I can "get your motor running … head out on the highway … looking for adventure … born to be wiiiildd", but after I've sung the chorus a few dozen times, I usually realise that knowing the words to songs is not my strength. Nor is song writing. I've tried that with a huge lack of success. I get writer's block immediately, and always my attempts are only pale rip-offs of others. Wife Stephanie sometimes reverts to her Baptist upbringing and belts out hymns at the top of her voice. Interestingly, a friend Janet does the same, and when we ride together often they excitedly compare what they've been singing at the end of the day.

But back to the past. I did stop and have a solitary beer at DeBretts and so earn another 23 points to go with the 57.50 I'd accumulated since leaving home on Friday. And then it got dark. Nobody's fault, it just did. There is a certain perverse enjoyment about thundering along in the dark on an old bike. You know that half the drivers who catch you up are wondering "what the hell is this?" Bessie was magnificent that night. I don't know the speed we travelled at because she doesn't have a speedo … not required for another 15 years after she was born. We were just a little slower than most cars but not scarily so. The thud of her single-cylinder engine smoothed out at highway speeds to be a lovely soothing purr. We were both having fun, partly perhaps knowing that, in the perception of some, we were being intrepid. Of course, in reality, this was what we were made for. A sporting BSA motorcycle was made to be ridden, and I was lucky enough to somehow have been chosen to ride her.

But remember the squeeze? After quite few hours in the saddle, even Steppenwolf couldn't boost my resilience. Fun as the ride was, it was hard work, and my thoughts began to wander onto "what would I really like to be riding?" I know that I have somehow ended up stuck in a time warp of some sort. I know that a modern bike would be so enjoyable in comparison to those I ride. The performance would be so wonderful, the comfort making an outing like this just seem like a walk in the park. But deep down, there is something that has now taken hold, and I just can't bring myself to capitulate and get a sensible and suitable bike. I can't really explain it, but I am stuck with riding the old shitters. Hell, only six months earlier, I had ridden half-way across the world on Bessie's stablemate, Penelope the old Panther. I couldn't suddenly get a modern bike. A ride like this would be

GESTATION

5

greeted with, "so you rode through the night ... the bike's got lights hasn't it ... what's the big deal?". So what would I really like to be riding? It would have to be old, to keep my street cred alive, but it would be nice to have performance ... not performance from the 1930's ... something that could crack the old 100 mph. I'd have to like it, and it would have to be reliable. I am not the sort to have fast but fragile or fussy bikes. Maintenance and polishing aren't my things.

Brother Roly has a 1000 cc Vincent, a thundering great two-miles-a-minute machine that bursts into life with an evocative and inspirational roar – a lusty crackle that still raises the hairs on my arms. I love the noise, I love the speed potential ... but it is not me. It is a bit of a pig to start, and I didn't enjoy my last ride on it in the wet. Fast but no cigar ... not suited. So bouncing up and down on my sprung saddle, I wondered ... and enjoyed wondering. I wasn't too cold, I wasn't too uncomfortable, I was sitting in the dark following a dancing pool of light thinking how happy I was, how much fun I was having. I think I have quite a low threshold for fun. A nine-hour ride on an old bike and I'm in clover, even when it is too small for me. Actually a quick blat around the block on anything with two wheels and I am happy ... this is just the same thing multiplied out a few hundred times. But what a difficult choice I was facing away in Fantasy Land. I wanted old but I wanted new. I'd ridden Bessie to Pukekohe twice before, and I wasn't sure if we'd do it again in 2007. I am a naturally loyal person but sometimes you have to move on ... or so I told myself. Although Fantasy Land has no price tags and no obstacles to procurement, I really struggled to find that dream steed that I'd like to be on. I'd seen all sorts of exotica in the last couple of days,, but some were too flashy, lots were too specialised, some were only fit for scrawny youths, some were just too common and easily achieved ... there has to be a bit of class involved when you are musing. The elimination process went on for many a long, dark mile and then almost like a song ... "somewhere near Marton Lord, I found my dream companion" ... the ultimate gentleman's express.

The best motorcycle I have ever owned, I reflected, had to be my 1959 BMW R60, a wonderfully soft tourer that was the ultimate in reliability and style. It had been quiet, it had been competent at everything, even on gravel, and probably best of all, I liked looking at it ... and to be honest, I liked others looking at it too. Steph and I had toured many a long mile, comfortably and happily. It wasn't fast, but it got along nicely at between 60 and 65 mph. Sadly, this bike had finally let me down with a broken crankshaft at approximately 300,000 miles. These weren't all of my doing but we'd certainly done more miles together than any of my other bikes at the time. I'd lamented her passing, but life went on. Now my real dream bike would be the same, same ... but faster. Yes, there is a sports version of the bike, called an R69S. I knew I'd seen one in a barn in Taupō once but was not aware of having laid eyes on any others. So it had the ingredient of being rare ... good start. Instead of the 30 BHP that the R60 produces, the R69S pumps out 42, which is a third more ... what a machine. I knew from a book I've had for 30 years that the top speed was 110, which was more than adequate for my dream machine. Cruise at 70, plenty on hand to pass the occasional caravan etc. I grinned at the thought ... I wonder how rare they really are? Where would you get one?

The enjoyment of thinking about the whisper-quiet, swift, stealthy, old-but-new dream bike kept me alive with buzzing thoughts for the last couple of hours. Suddenly I was being magically transported along on an elegant black and chrome (with white pin stripes) Teutonic masterpiece. The air-cooled horizontally-opposed twin-cylinder engine just humming along, the leading-link Earles fork front-end gently rising up and down in front of me in the eerily plush way they do ... quite unlike any other bike. A friend had called my old R60, "marshmallow wheels" because of the soft ride.

Bessie and I arrived home in the early hours, fairly spent but happy with our achievement. Silently, I thanked her for her sterling effort, and on pins-and-needles-affected unsteady legs, I went up the steps to bed. I knew that the body would soon shrug off the aches and pains, shoulder knots, tired forearms etc. and the fatigue would melt away.

Fantasy Land episodes like the 'dream bike' usually fade quite quickly, and my ever-erratic mind moves on to the next unobtainable flighty chapter. This one, however, was more persistent, and finally the thought of that wonderful BMW drove me into the powerful web-like clutches of eBay. I was only just going to have a look to see if there were any R69S BMWs for sale anywhere in the world. And bugger me ... there was. Over the years I reckon the strike rate of my fantasies is probably 1 in 1,000. Just because I had found an R69S for sale didn't mean I had to buy it ... although there was an overwhelming attraction. It really did seem to be the once-in-a-lifetime opportunity that rarely comes your way. This pristine 1965 gem seemed to be absolutely original with only 3,500 miles on the clock ... unbelievable. When my old R60 finally let me down, it was worn out from one end to the other. The brake drums were worn oversize, the drive pinions were flogged out, the cylinder heads cracked, timing gears had lost teeth and then a crank pin failed. This would be the complete opposite ... nothing had had the chance to wear out. It might be 41 years old, but it hadn't been doing anything for most of that time. The current owner had not ridden it despite having it for quite a few years. It had been started from time to time but that was all. The bike was in Michigan, a northern state of the US where the bikes have to be laid up for the winter every year and of course if you don't get off your bum to put in back on the road when the summer comes, you end up leaving it stored for another winter and so on. Wow!

I don't really want to describe the stomach-churning process that went on as I moved from 'would love that bike' to 'must have that bike' ... or the times later when aficionados of the marque from all over the world scrapped over the ether for it. Auctions are stressful at the best of times. With only Roly in on the action, I lived a tense couple of weeks waiting for the auction to close, and towards the end, it becomes fever pitch. You can scarcely breathe as you bid and 'refresh' the computer every few seconds to monitor your bid. Of course, there wouldn't be a story without the success of my bidding. It was hard to know if I paid too much, as there is no benchmark for such an offering, but ultimately it was mine. This isn't a time I want to dwell on, as it is not something I am really proud of because there was a bit of deception. I did all this without the approval of the immediate family … I was too scared to ask. So I owned my dream bike, now what to do with it? It was in Michigan and I was in New Zealand.

Even in real life, I have to confess to not being the greatest at completing one thing before I am distracted and off onto another thing. Well, in Fantasy Land, the same thing goes on. Other flights of fancy were taking me on a magic carpet ride again as dear, old Steppenwolf would sing. I had chronicled my *Last Hurrah* old-bike ride from Beijing to Arnhem in Holland, and a book was being produced by a small UK publisher. We also dreamed of putting together a DVD. What if … my head was asking … I could ride across the US on the old BMW promoting my book and DVD? That would make the bike a tool for good, not evil.

The weeks went by, the thoughts clarified and the dreams evolved and started to dovetail together. I'd owned up to buying the bike and feebly justified my irresponsible purchase as part of a master-plan to take my book and DVD worldwide. I started to try and plan a promotional campaign. My UK publisher Rollo Turner of Panther Publishing (not to be confused with my brother Roly) was very doubtful as there would be no pre-publicity to drum up any interest, and there was also concern that the book wouldn't be finished in time. It would be hard, he warned.

Daughter Kitty was keen to come away with me, and we'd make her the cameraperson this time. I was hoping to document the 'little Kiwi battler' taking on the US by way of a road trip. I'd poured over maps and looked at the myriad of routes that criss-cross the US like the tiny red veins in an old drunk's eye. It was bewildering and almost disheartening ... but just as dawn does finally come and slowly spread light into your day, so it was with this trip. Roly had been rereading *Zen and the Art of Motorcycle Maintenance* (ZAMM), the seminal book of the 1970s that had attained cult status in that era. We'd first read it during our youthful motorbike ride from New Orleans to Buenos Aires in 1976/77. Not really a book about Zen or motorcycle maintenance, the philosophy had been too deep for us then, but we loved the on-the-road adventure content. We reminisced about how hard the book was to read, and we talked of the Earles-forked 600 cc BMW that tagged along for part of the ride as being like the one I had just bought. I think it was also Roly who showed me a photo from a website dedicated to the book. We hadn't known it ... or thought much about it ... but the book was based on a real ride and 12 photos exist from it. The most evocative ... and the one that made the trip become what it did ... showed the author Robert Pirsig's bike to be a Honda 305 cc Super Hawk and it was parked in front of the BMW in what turned out to be a lay-by on the 11,000 ft Beartooth Pass in Montana. 12-year-old Chris Pirsig stands behind the luggage-laden bikes grinning, and the riders of the BMW, the Sutherlands, have their arms around each other, all of them overshadowed by snowy peaks and icy glaciers. Pirsig must have been behind the lens. Somehow the photo stirred the wanderer in me intensely, and suddenly I really wanted to be there, in that exact spot, with my BMW. It didn't take long for the dream to move into wanting to have a Honda in my photo too. "Eureka!" We'd recreate Pirsig's ride from his book. Up to this point, my planning had been confused and aimless. Now the research became focused. Quite easily, we tracked the *Zen* route from St Paul/Minneapolis to San Francisco. There was a good website that laid it out. ZAMM itself doesn't really give the route as it is not a travel book

... it is a book about philosophy. Fortunately, the book has spawned such interest that there are 'pilgrims' who have researched and traced out what they believe to be the route taken in 1968.

Even how *Zen and the Art of Motorcycle Maintenance* came into being is the stuff of legend – the sort of thing that my dreaming self could relish and identify with. 121 publishers turned Robert Pirsig down before one finally said, "This is why I am in publishing," commenting that they'd never recover costs but "go off and finish it anyway!" The book went on to sell five million copies, the most popular philosophy book of all time. The introduction to a piece I wrote about the ride explains:

In July 1968 a mentally insecure philosophy professor began a motorcycle ride across the US with his not yet 12-year-old son. His name was Robert Pirsig, and the journey from St Paul across to San Francisco was immortalized in his subsequent best-selling book Zen and the Art of Motorcycle Maintenance. *His focus on the metaphysics of quality and the deep philosophical arguments have led the book to be referenced as required reading across a broad spectrum of university degrees ranging from Engineering through English to Sociology, Physics, Psychology and Philosophy. Although it has been a hugely popular book with many proponents claiming it has changed their lives and the way they look at things, for most it is a difficult and very challenging read. The philosophies are often deep and confusing as he challenges thinking dating back to Socrates – usually through his other persona Phaedrus. All this cerebral activity is interwoven with an epic road trip, told with clarity and a disarming frankness. Pirsig tells the tale with what appears to be truthfulness even when at times it makes him seem almost cruel to those around him.*

Now that I had a good clear goal to chase, it seemed suddenly to be easier ... if you overlooked the fact that we didn't have a finished book, a DVD, a 1964-65 Honda Super Hawk or another suitable companion. My first choices were out. Legendary travelling mate from *The Last Hurrah* Dick Huurdeman, was not well enough to embark on such a journey, and son Steve who'd been the cameraman and general factotum on that ride, had gone away to East Timor doing research for his master's in environmental planning. On his return, he'd be frantically juggling his thesis and helping with the production of our DVD. There was no way he could duck off again for another 6 weeks or so.

I wanted someone who would gel with both Kitty and I. Of course, I think I am easy to get along with (although I would say that …) as I don't fret about things too much and I tend to see things as being at least half full (usually three-quarters full, in fact), not half empty. Possibly I am a bit too optimistic, but I am known as being pretty transparent and tolerant. What you see is what you get. I know I lack real drive and the intensity that goes with it, but there is no moodiness in my life and that has never worried me or the others who are close to me.

Kitty at nearly 22 has arrived at a nice time in her life, being a lovely mix of caring adult, coupled with youthful naivety and passion. At times ,it has been a bumpy road getting there, with many highs and lows … although it has always been an interesting journey. A lover of music, she'd been the drummer in an anarcho-feminist punk band, she'd left home early to go do a Diploma in Contemporary Music. She followed this with a massage therapy qualification from another institution. She does Reiki and reflexology, she has studied yoga to higher plane (if you get what I mean) and is quite spiritual. She has spent time with Buddhists and the Hare Krishna, and she is still an animal activist, rabid vegetarian and strong feminist. In the past, her strong views have clashed with those of us who lack her zeal and commitment. She has had the waist-long dreadlocks, but now has an almost shaven-headed boyish style that complements her lean figure and often wispy hippie clothes.

With a proposed journey that was way beyond just taking a few days' annual leave, it could have been hard to find someone who fitted my criteria and who was available and willing. Surprisingly, it turned out to be remarkably simple. I thought of Myles Feeney because I felt he'd be interesting to be on the road with. He'd traveled, he is a reader, someone who has never had a television set in the house, his daughters were of a similar age as ours and he is self-employed, which I felt could enable a mid-year escape. I just felt also that he'd fit well with Kitty. He wouldn't judge her ways or be condescending towards her lack of worldliness and experience. I enjoyed his dry wit and knew that I would enjoy finding out more about his interesting past. Myles is a builder who sometimes does work at the building research facility where I work as a technical writer and seminar presenter. Although we had enjoyed many a smoko break (and Friday beers) together and he'd joined the classic motorbike club that I was part of, we didn't really know much about each other. We were of a similar age and background, but that was the limit of our contact to date.

We often now laugh at my delusion, as I even felt we were of a similar, slightly corpulent body shape. This reality was shattered after I borrowed his leather jacket for a TV interview (my motorcycling gear was still in transit from Holland), later smirking and smugly passing off the jibe that he'd never get into that jacket as it was even a little snug on me. The graphic demonstration that he could slip into it with room to spare, was a sad day for me but it has led to the catch-call of "remember when I was skinnier than Myles?", which always brings the scoffing rebuttal that it probably deserves.

Myles had been very enthusiastic about my last adventure, passing the comment once that he'd love to do something like that. So it was that when I went to him with an apparent flight of fancy, he hardly batted an eyelid, just asking, "When are we starting?" I knew that, with a push, the book and DVD should both be ready by mid-July 2006. A quick look at the timing had shown me that the biggest gathering of motorcyclists in the world takes place each year in a small South Dakota town called Sturgis and it would be in early to mid-August. This seemed a good place to sell a book and DVD about motorcycling ... or so I thought. I also learned of the American Motorcycle Association's Vintage Days at the Mid-Ohio Raceway near Lexington, Ohio, which is held each year at the end of July. It seemed easy to link both and additionally do the *Zen* ride, as Sturgis was only just a small detour off Pirsig's route and we'd do Mid-Ohio before we got out of the Michigan area on the way to the starting point of St Paul in Minnesota

The BMW was in Dearborn and fortuitously the family of Shauna, an exchange student we'd had a few years back lived only 20 miles away in Ypsilanti. Even more fortuitously, her parents Pat and Sandy were both motorcycle enthusiasts and I'd kept contact with them even after Shauna had moved from our lives to have one of her own with motherhood and further study. It hadn't taken much arm twisting for them to agree to store the bikes until our visit. The magic of eBay enabled me to find a low-mileage 1965 CB 77 Honda in South Carolina. After a bit of hesitation, we decided that the 'buy now' price wasn't over the top, and even though the owner had 'lost' the title, it would be better to have a bike in the hand rather than to be still searching as the countdown began. It was white and chrome, whereas Pirsig's was black and chrome, but as I'd gone down a few deadends in the search, it'd do. Accordingly, Myles transferred the required funds, and we arranged to have the bike transported to Michigan so we could have them both prepared for the journey. "Phew" it was really beginning to happen.

I now marvel at how easy it all looks as I write down the processes. It seems you just go on eBay, get two bikes, magically make them appear where you want to start the ride ... hey presto, bloody simple. Let's leave it at that, as the details are all just too hard to explain and now quite irrelevant. Although the bikes were like the originals they differed in one important way. They were now over 40 years old. Sure they might be quite low-mileage examples, but they still needed to be carefully prepared for the journey. Suitable artisans were fortunately found, and our man on the ground Pat c-oordinated this getting under way.

On our side of the world, we struggled, finding it hard to know what sort of venues would be suited for a book promotion and DVD screenings. As we didn't know anything about the towns we were going to travel through, this isn't surprising, although at the time nothing seemed unreasonable. The further time went on, the harder it seemed to get. We did manage to book a spot at the Mid-Ohio Vintage Days for the three days as part of the swap meet though. We'd be one of 1,000 stalls peddling our wares, and then a couple of weeks later we were to have a place at a large campground in Sturgis. It didn't sound ideal, but at least we could afford it. Getting a rented spot on Main Street Sturgis, was definitely out of the question.

It should be pointed out that at this point in time there were not yet wares for us to sell. There was no book, there was no DVD. I felt I had done my bit … I'd laid down the words. After a month's rest at journey's end, I had put my head down and written. I had written almost at every waking moment that I wasn't at work. I don't pretend to be a driven man with huge energy levels and extreme focus, so this was quite out of character. The kids likened me to a chipmunk the way I sat in front of the computer and pecked away – not that we have chipmunks in New Zealand, so they've never actually seen one. Chipmunking became what I did in my spare time. When asked what I'd be getting up to on any given weekend, evening etc. I'd reply "chipmunking". As an indication of the size of the chipmunking that needed to be done, if I wrote 1,000 words that I was pleased with on any one night, it was quite a sobering thought that I'd have to do that nearly 100 times. But that is what I did. 5,000 words became 10,000 then 15,000 and finally 90,000. I barely paused for breath.

Almost unbelievably, I had the first draft finished not long after Christmas 2005. For three months, I had chipmunked my heart out. I'd had no social life, no spare time, but it was done. Rollo was very surprised and indicated that he didn't want me to do anything with the manuscript until he came out to New Zealand in February. This should have left me with free time to work on the DVD, but somehow I was spent, mentally as much as physically. Son Steve who had filmed the adventure had left me the tapes when he went off to East Timor. He returned in March to find I'd done nothing with the tapes and yet was planning a promotional tour of the US in July. Being the action man that he is, he uplifted the tapes, returned to university in Dunedin and advertised on their 'student job search' for a film editor to help him make a movie.

Fortunately, then Katrina Jones, a young film maker, came into our lives. About to graduate from the New Zealand Natural History Film Unit, she was finishing her own project on our iconic bird the tūī, but was still very keen to be involved. Rumour has it that she had crashed her boyfriend's car and was pretty keen to earn some extra money to pay off the damage caused. This turned out to be a bonus for us.

Say it quickly and it is always easy. Rollo came and took the manuscript away while he holidayed in the South Island, returning with encouraging words. Learning of my plans, he expressed doubt that things could be done so quickly, and there were also a couple of books ahead of mine in the line to be published. This led me to take over the responsibility of organising the editing, graphics and general layout of the book. Rollo's Panther Publishing would only have to do the final check and arrange for the printing, which was going to be done in Malta.

Soon I had done my stuff, cousin Elspeth had done the first edit, work contacts Ruth and David had done the layout and graphics, Kitty's boyfriend Cam had done the maps and finally Myles had done the proofreading. Rollo approved, fine-tuned and gave the printers an urgent go, go, go. He also arranged for 500 books to be sent by air to me as they came off the presses and a similar number to be sent to Michigan to await our arrival. I then set in stone a premiere and book launch for Sunday night 15 July 2006. All the while, I was busy and committed with my work as a writer and presenter for BRANZ, New Zealand's building research facility. Belatedly, I had been asked to do a six-week nationwide series of presentations on building stuff, which wouldn't end until after I was supposed to leave for the US. As with most successful resolutions, a bit of give and take was needed. I'd shorten my trip by a week, and the presentations would be done without me for a week. This was deemed to be OK. We'd have the premiere on Sunday, Kitty and Myles would head for Michigan the next day, and I would carry on spreading the good word for my employer for another week before heading away on Monday the 24th after completing the last 'important' seminar in Auckland that day.

For short periods, it is amazing what can be sustained in the way of enthusiasm if the inspiration is there. Myles got involved with some of the planning, and probably we would have had better results if he'd been given more of a free hand. It was frustrating that so much was in my head and couldn't always be accessed easily. Myles arranged some stunning silk-screened banners and a weather balloon that would have a large printed promotional 'cummerbund' around its middle. The idea was that we'd inflate it with helium, and the photos and logos would float above the crowds and hopefully attract them like bees around a honey pot. In the spirit of a journey done in the late 1960s, Myles decided he would use an old Trapper Nelson pack to carry a lot of his luggage. He also asked could he bring a Thermette. My standard response to this sort of question is "if you can carry it you can bring it." Whilst the Thermette is an iconic New Zealand water boiling device, it is the sort of thing Pirsig would have taken if he'd had one.

The Thermette is a wonder of simplicity that warrants an explanation.

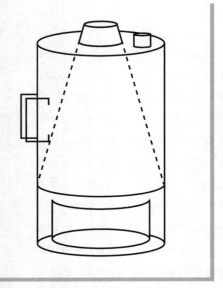

There is a cylindrical spacer about five inches high where a fire is made under the boiler unit which is about 12 inches high and of the same diameter on the outside, with an inside that tapers down to the two-inch chimney that projects through the top. This makes a conical water jacket that is top filled through what is the pouring spout. A couple of fold-out wire handles complete the package. Because the water jacket completely surrounds the fire and goes from a thin point that heats quickly (and hot water rises), it is incredibly efficient as the tapered chimney makes the fire and smoke pass through quickly, creating a low-pressure area that draws more air in through the bottom, further feeding the fire. A small fire is started using almost anything, then once under way, it is top fed through the chimney. Leaves, twigs and small broken branches can be poked in. In an amazingly short time, enough water for 12 cups of tea is boiled. When finished with, the fire can be extinguished with a small splash of water. This leaves just a small four- inch blackened circle to show that you have been there. This wonderful device was invented by John Ashley Hart in 1929, and patented in 1931 – originally being promoted by the slogan "the more the wind, the quicker it boils". In 1939, the Government on behalf of the Army asked Mr Hart to waive the patent rights. Accordingly, they got approval to make and supply their troops in the North African deserts. From this came the nickname Benghazi boiler and the reputation as the quickest boiler there was. Every sixth soldier was issued with one. Later still, apprentice plumbers were required to make one as part of their demonstration of sheet metal skills. Still made and sold today, the older copper ones like Myles brought along are in high demand on the internet auction sites.

Meanwhile, posters were made, a movie theatre was booked, wine and nibbles were arranged and information was spread around furiously. We were trying to simultaneously plan a local extravaganza, organise our bikes in the US and detail a promotional ride and *Zen* ride recreation. Did that mean we did none of them well? Probably. We were struggling with the US side of things. In my head, I thought I knew what type of venue I wanted, but unlocking this for Kitty to find and get to them, was proving impossible. Motorbike clubs also seemed hard to contact and didn't usually have clubrooms or meet very often. Our contacts on the ground didn't quite have the 'know' needed. This was no fault of theirs. We really needed a publicist, but that is not a world we know anything of, and we didn't know how to get one suited to our needs. In typical Kiwi fashion, we felt we would manage it all on our own. I mean … how hard can it be?

Making contact with BMW and Honda America was also proving impossible. We'd thought they might be interested in our plan, seeing as we'd be riding nice examples of their products that had survived the test of time, but we managed nowt. Their websites were just set up for encouraging sales, not actually contacting them. In fact, both corporations seemed to make it impossible to find out how to talk to them or write to them. There was a moment when we thought we were going to possibly get the opportunity to speak with Ford employees in Dearborn, Michigan, as my BMW's owner had put all the arranging in the hands of Dennis, a friend of hers who just happened to be part of middle management in Ford. Disappointingly, it came to nothing. Again, close but no cigar.

Meanwhile, Steve and Katrina soldiered on in their spare time putting together a movie. I wasn't consulted or interviewed other than meeting Katrina before they started. Their project had a life of its own. Time went on, and Pete Gorman, another talented person, came on board to help with the sound and graphics. Reports kept coming back to me that progress was OK but the timing was a bit tight. That worried me a bit, but I had enough other things to worry about ... I was trying again to read ZAMM. I've always felt that my failure to connect with the book was due to us being a bit young and immature for the topic when we read it in 1977. This time, I told myself, I could take as long as I liked and really read it. I have to say I did better this time but still couldn't help moving on past the deep stuff to get back to the ride ... because it is so damn good. For me, it captures the spirit of being on the road so well. My thoughts are just like Pirsig's. I too love the backroads – I love the vistas. His descriptions of car drivers' views are just how I would describe them. I too do a lot of thinking when I am riding ... I just don't challenge thinking all the way back to Socrates. It is interesting that Amazon Books shows ZAMM as having an extremely high level of product dissatisfaction. There are those who will write that the book changed their lives and the way they looked at things. A friend wrote just that when he learned of the ride I was planning. Others just bog down and find it all too hard. Motorcyclists are looking for one thing and *Zen* followers are looking for another, and probably both will be disappointed. This is not a once-over-lightly read. For all but the ultimate theorists, this is as deep as it gets.

I gave Myles the book to read, and his overwhelming response was how hard Pirsig was on young Chris. I half agreed but felt that his absolute honesty was admirable. He was never going to come out of this book as the good guy. Young Chris for me is the hero, whilst Pirsig and his alter ego Phaedrus are very self-indulgent know-alls. I could feel Myles's point. As a parent, Pirsig wasn't very understanding. He was self-destructing for half of the book ... but more of that later. I felt that showing his human weaknesses and obvious failings was quite courageous, whereas Myles just thought he was a bastard.

One thing has always irritated the shit out of me. It is the inaccuracy of the cover on the edition I have. One of the central themes to ZAMM is the metaphysics of quality, yet there on the cover is a spanner morphing into the lotus blossom leaves of peace. The spanner shown is an imperial AF (American Fine) one, which could not be used on either of the motorcycles used on the journey. The inaccuracy of this cover for me is inexcusable. I recall being mortified when my graphic designer showed a metric spanner on the draft cover of *The Last Hurrah*. I told him I'd never live it down if it was left like that. It had to be changed to an imperial Whitworth spanner, because they were the only spanners that could be used on the motorbikes used on that adventure. The designer said, "does it matter?", and my answer was in capital letters: "OF COURSE IT DOES!" I know Pirsig would have had nothing to do with the book's cover, especially when my copy is a paperback ... but it does demonstrate a complete lack of what he often advocates in ZAMM. Early in the book, he rails against the drop in standards and lack of caring at a motorcycle shop, where he was having some work done on his bike. To me, the cover illustration exhibits that same lack of accuracy.

Looking back, it is hard to recall whether time flew by during the preparation or whether it crawled along ... because it does seem that we put together a lot in a short time. Suddenly, it was the day of the book launch and movie premiere. The books had arrived with plenty of days to spare. One copy had been taken from the stock and ceremonially delivered to Dick, another given to friend who would be travelling on the night, the rest were locked away for the special occasion. Steve, Katrina and Pete arrived from Dunedin on the actual day with a nearly finished movie, and it all panned out beautifully. The night was chaotic but wonderful. The team finished the movie with 30 minutes to go before the curtain was to go up ... the 500-seat theatre was sold out, the street outside was lined with motorcycles, beyond what we could have dreamed of. New and old bikes filled Courtenay Place and new and old motorcyclists poured in the doors, past Penelope and Dutch Courage, the stars of the show. It was scary but

A Motorcycle Odyssey

Join Des, Dick and Steve (with their bikes Penelope and Dutch Courage) for the DVD screening and book launch:

Where: **The Paramount Theatre**
25 Courtney Place
Wellington

When: **Sunday July 16th 2006**

Time: **6.00 pm** for a 6.45 pm curtain

Bookings: Email – des@thelasthurrah.co. nz or
Email – paramount@paramount.co.nz or
Phone – Paramount Theatre, Ph: 04 384 4080

Cost: **Only $20**
including wine and
finger food

thrilling. A who's who of Wellington's bike world presented themselves for the occasion. Later I stood in front of the seated throng and professed my trepidation as I hadn't yet seen the movie and Katrina hadn't read the book. I worried needlessly.

A wonderful night followed, giving rise to effusive praise for the movie and good book sales making it worthwhile. Of course, it could have been the 90 bottles of wine we provided for the after-match function. With Steve following on Bessie, it was a euphoric little procession that finally gunned their old bikes away home after all was finished. The still night air seemed receptive to the staccato bark of our three British single-cylinder bikes being taken on a triumphant ride out home behind the Russian Ural sidecar outfit of friend Michael. It seemed a fitting end to the night to speed through the deserted streets, laughing.

And just like that ... it was over. Kitty and Myles flew away the next day, whilst I went back on the road, telling the construction world about masonry construction. It seemed a long week as I travelled about New Zealand, longing to know how the team was getting on in the US. Reports soon filtered back that not all was going swimmingly. The books and banners were there, but neither bike was yet fully prepared and ready to go. Myles was struggling with the Michigan way of putting things off ... of 'not' doing things. He sees things clearly, prioritises well and as a builder, is used to deciding on a task and doing it ... end of story. Not easily distracted, he just wanted to get the insurances sorted out, the legal titles established, the bikes finished. From the other side of the world, I couldn't understand the problems. Eight days later, I gave my last presentation and headed for Auckland Airport, family farewells having had to be done a couple of days earlier. Soon I was in the air with my trusty Palm One PDA pocket computer on my lap siting in the cradle of the fold-out keyboard and writing.

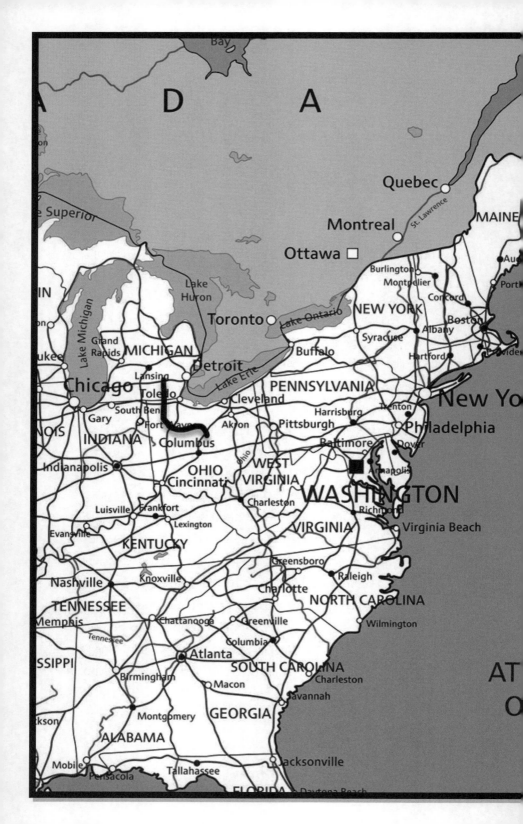

Chapter Two

AFTERBIRTH

Again I start an adventure in an aeroplane, with of course lots of time for reflection. For some reason, air travel is seen as exotic. It is exciting for sure because of what it promises, but the conduit to that dream is a squashed alien world. It is a test of endurance. There are long periods of sitting, elbows in, without sleep. There are the short periods with sleep, ending when your body rejects the cramp-inducing position that you felt sure would be more comfortable than the last cramp-inducing position.

Sometimes there are the loud bores nearby. I've suffered car bores, travel bores, children bores, financial bores and techno bores that I can easily recall. Sometimes there have been whining ill-disciplined kids, often being admonished by adults patently not suited to be parents. Flying also shows up your level of technical adaptability. Nobody explains how to use the corded remote that is hidden in your armrest … or what it can do. Nobody shows you how to drain the basin in the cupboard that doubles as a toilet or how to flush the thing. These are all part of some huge aptitude test.

Probably the biggest test comes when your meal arrives on a tray almost as big as your fold-down table. All the food is packaged, which necessitates careful unpackaging and care, with elbows now up in the only space available to you. You then realise that there is nowhere to put the wrappings etc., so you try and balance them on top of the bits you aren't eating at the time. There should be night classes training us how to do this. The challenge of feeding yourself, without applying food to your clothing, is *one that I again failed. This time it was apple and Manuka-honey syrup, which I had applied over my French toast. So again I'll arrive in stained clothes, but thank God it wasn't the coffee this time ... and the stain is in a more acceptable place.*

At least being able to peck away on my Palm One filled in some time and provided an immediate record for later reference. Travel is something that does expose you to the unusual, even in places like LA Airport, which I wouldn't have rated high on my exotica scale. I remember from my last crossing of the US 30 years ago how big American people can be. Well, they haven't shrunk – there are still lots and lots of fat folk out there scoffing McD's. There are also the amazingly beautiful and different looking people. Walking through the airport in their summer skimpy gear were two women who must have been close to 6 feet tall in old money. They had film-star looks but with tattoos totally covering their bodies, even emerging from places we can only imagine. They strode through the concourse like a mobile freak show.

Later, I passed another young woman who was in severe danger of falling out of her dress. There was no way she could run if she was late. What they thought of this out-of-place stumbling Kiwi wearing his motorbike jacket, and carrying a helmet, a full tank bag and another open bag full of books, DVDs and Myles's all-important Stuyvesant Lights, we'll never know ... just another part of that freak show probably.

The NorthWest flight from LA to Detroit was budget with very little service and nearly a bit of 'plane rage' as a very hassled-looking woman with two kids couldn't find anywhere to put her stuff. One guy had a guitar in the locker and didn't want anything on It ... and then another guy had a small low box that he wouldn't let her add to either. In frustration, she called out to the attendant ... and he viciously admonished her for shouting at him. Others were saying she should have boarded earlier.

Before boarding, I had sat with a sweet old African American lady who needed a wheelchair to take her onto the plane. We had a few laughs as they kept getting it wrong and wanting to take her away. She did make the flight though and called out as I passed. I was also pleased to be aboard, as there had been dramas with luggage on the LA flight nearly going off to London ... and as a result, there had been delays. Later, just like Myles and Kitty a week earlier, my gear was searched. A small moment of consternation was experienced as the officer put on rubber gloves ... and we've all heard about rubber glove searches! But no, he probably just doesn't like fossicking through people's dirty clothes without protection. You never know what you'll catch.

And so it was that, at midnight on 24 July, I finally reached Detroit, dirty and knackered. The smiling faces of Kitty and Myles met me, and lurking away to one side was our Michigan host Pat McNally, who I had corresponded with for six years. Open-faced, rotund, jovial and a very humble working-class American, Pat was patient and unfazed by being in Detroit in the middle of the night. When you're tired, things always seem to take a long time, and the wait for my luggage to appear on the carousel was interminable. It was like being back in childhood days where you get picked from a line-up by popularity to go in a team. You're eager to be picked, but somehow you keep unfairly getting left to the end. Everybody else seemed to be getting to dart forward and pick up their luggage and scuttle away. Ever so slowly, the magic luggage roundabout gave up its goodies. Finally, there were just a couple of us rejects left ... the ones who the luggage didn't want. We weren't even wanted in the team as the dummies who'd get out first, no matter what the activity. Forlornly, we watched the empty conveyor for a while as it snaked along like an enormous and continuous liquorice strap. Finally, all hope was lost. There were no more bags cruising along the rubber ribbon looking for someone to choose. Dejectedly, we straggled over to a lost-luggage window, and I gave Pat's details to the generally disinterested and eager-to-go-home attendant.

Pat then soon had us in his very suburban stereotypical Chevy van, heading off on the 20 miles or so to Ypsilanti. The night was hot, but the new and changing environment was the stimulation needed to perk me up. No longer was I a prisoner in the big silver bird, squashed in with reticent strangers, being intermittently fed and watered like a human battery hen. Kitty chirped away excitedly, the CD player threw out Tom Petty at us and the van thumped along the high-level freeway, the expansion joints rhythmically interjecting. Even fatigued and with the knowledge that the bikes weren't ready and there was no set-in-concrete time frame for them to be so ... I was happy. In the darkness, I grinned, in my head yet again I could hear a booming baritone voice proclaiming, "Let the games begin!" The adventure was about to happen. *Zen and the Last Hurrah* might not quite be up and running, but the die was cast. All the participants were in the same place, and the familiarity of home and hearth was far, far away. The rounding of each new corner had the potential to surprise, delight, disappoint, enthral or bore. We'd only find out by going there.

Sandy was still up and waiting to rekindle the easy companionship we'd shared during her visit to New Zealand, five or so years earlier. We'd loved her then, striking up a close friendship, and it was such a nice end of a long journey to be reunited and reflect on how our paths had crossed.

When our Joe was 17 he went on a year's exchange to Spain with a group called Youth For Understanding, which also ran shorter exchanges for American kids. They came for six weeks only and spent four weeks of that travelling around New Zealand in a bus and two weeks with a family. Often large corporate sponsors like Kellogg's enabled this to happen. We'd had a young lad called Eric from Kalamazoo, which had gone well, and I laugh when I recall hearing Steph on the phone the next year, saying "Well, I suppose so, a vegan you say" and I remember calling out, "No, no not the vegan!" Shauna had been the one hard-to-place exchange. Soon we had her bio, showing her to be a real strong character – not only a vegan but a wrestler, an activist on all sorts of issues and obviously a very clever, thoughtful, stroppy young woman. Shauna turned out to be all of that and more. She was not in the least bit daunted by being on the other side of the world at the age of 18 … she revelled in it. She demanded to go to school with Steve, our 17-year-old, and obviously enjoyed the 'exotic' status of being the centre of attention there. She took every opportunity and grasped it with two hands. She managed to inveigle her way into the Wellington High School formal ball, she bungee jumped, jet boated and rounded it all off by getting a tattoo … phew. She loved her time in New Zealand and decided that it would be cheaper and more fun to go to university there, and so it was that the following year Shauna returned with Sandy to help her settle into the apartments that now act as halls of residence for students of Victoria University.

We loved the 'normality' of Sandy. She was a middle-aged ordinary preschool teacher. She didn't have the mile-wide '60s Cadillac grille' smile of American TV moms. She didn't look like she'd had a facelift or a breast enhancement, she looked just like us … ordinary, showing the ordinary ravages of time … just like us. Which is probably why we liked her … not too big, not too small … just right. It was quite obvious that international travel to exotic locales was not the norm for Sandy, and we enjoyed showing her stuff because she was so appreciative. We took her out to our favourite art-house movie theatre. She couldn't believe that we could get real coffee there in real cups and just walk into the theatre with it. "Won't people steal the cups?" she fretted. It was a lovely night as the movie was an Irish one, about as far away in genre as you could get from the pap that Hollywood foists on the American public. We'd had another outing where we ended up at a café at a small farmlet where we'd seen most of the animals that feature in New Zealand's landscape. A piano there just begged Shauna to play it. It was nice to be with a mother/daughter pairing who for now were at ease with each other, and Sandy beamed with pride as Shauna banged away on the piano with considerable panache and enjoyment. All too soon, Sandy was summoned home as Pat had had a medical event that wasn't quite life threatening, but Sandy knew her place really was at his side – not half a world away enjoying herself.

During this time, I'd established a writing friendship with Sandy and Pat as they both loved their motorcycling and in particular motorcycle racing. We would compare thoughts on who was doing the business in World Superbike Racing. They had taken on Kiwi Aaron Slight as someone to support and cheer on. They'd met him at a US round of the championship and had collected autographed memorabilia etc. He was their link with New Zealand. They were also responsible for a very generous and spooky occurrence. My old BMW R60 had languished with its run big-end for many years, before I had an opportunity to swap this dead motorcycle for a live going one, albeit one of less status. This was great, as I felt that the 1958 350 cc Triumph 3TA would be an ideal bike for Steph to have (She hadn't had one since we sold her 250 cc BSA C11G Boadicea to replace our dead washing machine).

The swap was made, and whilst returning home with the Triumph on a trailer behind, I turned to Roly, and as part of the idle chatter that fills up the miles, I told him about the unexpected huge success The Art of the Motorcycle exhibition had been at the Guggenheim Museum in New York. He'd not been aware of this, and we talked a little about it and wondered what the content would have been. Two days later, a large carton arrived from Amazon, the book people. This had to be something big as the box measured 15 inches long, 12 inches wide and 3 inches thick. Totally bemused, I opened the box to find the coffee-table book *The Art of the Motorcycle* published by the Guggenheim Museum. Amazed as I was, I became even more astonished when this beautiful tome fell open to a delightful colour picture of … a 1958 Triumph 3TA. Spooky! There was no clue as to who it was from as it hadn't been sent from Michigan. A long time later, I learned it was indeed from Sandy and Pat. A wonderful and appreciated gift and just another eerie coincidence that life throws at us all from time to time.

The few days in Ypsilanti readying for the 'off' were frustrating, as everything seemed to have a confusing complexity. Our first job was to get the DVD replicated. The US has a different DVD format to the rest of the world, and we'd arranged to have them done by Russell Video Services in neighbouring Ann Arbor. For the reason only known to the 'destroying good ideas God', the master copy we had sent ahead hadn't beaten us to the facility. Fortunately, as a back-up, I had carried with me a couple more NTSC masters, and the helpful staff at Russell's bent over backwards to make it happen for us immediately so we could make our Mid-Ohio appointment in two days' time. Both bikes were coming along and almost ready. The BMW was being prepared by Kevin, a fascinating character who probably was working a little under the radar, being based at his home and liking things to be cash. He also wasn't too keen to appear in any movie footage. He was lean, almost to the point of concern, and he had a very lived-in face that told a million tales of a past that probably couldn't be remembered. Not a man for early mornings, we liked him and his slow, husky drawl. He oozed confidence and knew his old BMWs well. By now, he had carried out most of my instructions, which had been emailed to Pat. The workshop was immaculate, and that is often a clue to an ordered mind. We mused that Pirsig would have thought so anyway. The woodpile outside had a symmetry that hinted at fanaticism, drawing a chuckle from us and a photo.

Our Pat was another who wasn't an early-morning man, which had been a little frustrating to Myles who is. During the week prior to me getting there, Myles was purchasing all the things we needed to set up and sell at Mid-Ohio. Of course, to get around, he needed a navigator and driver who was Pat. For Myles, it always seemed they had to go across half the

state to get what was needed ... and usually the day was half gone before they would start. By the time I arrived, they had established a routine of bullying. Myles would bully Pat, who seemed to almost enjoy the 'victim' status. He'd had it in the army – "Yes sir, right away sir!" – and living with two women, especially one as strong as Shauna, had meant that he was inclined to defer to a position of subservience quite happily. Their roles had slowly become defined. Myles was decisive and good with logistics and planning, used to making things happen, whereas Pat was used to being told what to do. It worked well, even if the speed of achievement was less than Myles would have liked.

We seemed to have a circuit that we followed of going to the BMW, going to the DVD place, then the Honda shop and usually the motor-home place as well. There were also multiple trips to RadioShack and Walmart and insurance people etc. There was very little time for sightseeing. Ypsilanti is like many North American towns in that it is not at all suited for walking or cycling. Despite that, we would walk into the local suburban centre to the Post Office and grocery shop, and Kitty and I enjoyed a nice cycle ride one morning to a beautiful park, which I think had been donated by Ford many years earlier. The tardy starts to the day allowed this, which was a kind of bonus.

No one seemed to be able to explain to us the requirements for outsiders owning a motorcycle in the US and having it insured there. We also struggled with the concept of titles and tags a bit. We'd been getting nowhere fast with Myles's legal side as he didn't have any title to the Honda, and whilst there are companies in the US who specialise in getting these situations resolved ... they all seemed to have very confusing websites and none were close to hand. Finding someone who would insure us was also a little fraught. I wouldn't say we told lies, but we did have to stretch the truth slightly. I know Pat was a little hesitant, as at times we had to use his persona and address to enable paperwork to be completed. Being able to tick the right boxes and fill in the right fields on the computer seemed paramount, and there wasn't a scenario anything like ours in the guidance books. I seem to recall that not being able to insured so we could go into Canada almost derailed us, but late on Wednesday afternoon, we managed to get the plate and papers from The Secretary of State for the BMW. One down, one to go.

Oddly enough, America, which has so much bureaucracy, seems to have no safety check for vehicles. You have to have legal title, and you have to have the car or motorbike registered and that's it. Presumably, if it is found to be unsafe, you can be held responsible (and/or someone will sue the knickers off you), but there isn't a designated regular safety inspection as there is in the UK and NZ. This seemed odd as we'd pose the questions to ourselves, "How do they know the bike is safe? ... How do they know the brakes work? ... How do they know the steering-head bearings aren't flogged out or wrongly adjusted?" We were happy with the

way both bikes were being prepared – it was just a little frustrating that we weren't quite as ready as we would have liked. The BMW was picked up and found to be almost as I remembered my similar R60. The only concern was that the seat didn't have the support to keep my posture right, making it uncomfortable to ride for long periods. This was ultimately resolved by positioning a partially inflated Thermarest sleeping pad on the seat, and that worked a treat.

Myles and I did a ride out together on the BMW, and I managed to get us hopelessly lost. It was a lovely afternoon, and we meandered along in confusion, ultimately riding down a leafy, winding, riverside backroad and having to stop at a country store for help. Expecting Myles to give me a bit of stick for the poor navigation and the position we found ourselves in, I was delighted by his proclamation that it was "a great day to be lost and a great place to be lost in".

Our plan for the ride across the US was still blurred. We didn't have any *Last Hurrah* promotional opportunities laid out ahead, apart from Mid-Ohio and Sturgis. Logistically, we only the roughest idea of how we were going to even make that happen. Pat had a large motor-home, and I had felt that if he would tag along carrying all the books, DVDs, the gazebo, chairs, banners etc., we could use it for accommodation and save costs even if there was a price to pay for having another vehicle along and a decision would have to be made when to send it back. Sturgis? The motor-home was a thirsty beast, but there didn't seem to be any other way. Accordingly, Pat had been readying the behemoth while we were getting the bikes going. His preparation seemed to consist of buying all sorts of cleaners and greases for the rubber bushes that the side compartments slide out on. For something that you would have thought you just drove off in, a lot of work had to go into it. As we constantly needed Pat, the completion of his seen-to-be-necessary chores got later and later. We recognised that this was his baby, and he had a routine and nothing was going to change or short-circuit it. It would be done when it was done. Sandy and Pat do a lot of camping and enjoy their motor-home, even though it had been a huge financial drain and they had been trying unsuccessfully to sell the beast for some months.

Myles and Kitty had realised after arriving that we were really a huge imposition as there was a lot going on in the McNally household and we shouldn't have been adding to the stresses. Much had happened in Shauna's life since her New Zealand time, and she was now a solo mum of two small children, she was doing medical studies, working as well, and had just returned home, prior to going to Mexico to continue her path to being a doctor. Sandy had retired earlier in the year and was more or less doing full-time childcare while Shauna worked and studied. Sandy would also be going to Mexico in the short term. Their departure was looming, and there were nervous tensions that were evident. Shauna was still a young dynamic party-girl who was about to go away from her friends etc., so she was taking every opportunity to take her farewell in style and often. This would put more strain on the family dynamics, and Sandy wasn't the relaxed, happy person I remembered. She was often on edge, appearing to be worn down by the pending upheavals. There were only glimpses of the old Sandy, usually in the evenings, when a beer was in hand and the grandkids were otherwise occupied. She would then unwind the coiled spring that she'd become. We did have one nice, relaxing, fun night when we went to a local Mexican restaurant to celebrate Sandy and Pat's 35th wedding anniversary. Everybody was together, and the night flowed accordingly. You can't plan a night to be good, it just happens, and this one was nice.

The weather was hot across the US as it often is each summer. They give you the temperature two ways on the TV. They give you the actual reading, which might be 96 degrees Fahrenheit. They also give the humidity, then they give you a resulting composite figure. So a 96 degree day with a high humidity will possibly get over 100 degrees in a 'what it feels like' figure. Strange but true. Not really sure if it matters, as I am a strong believer that there are two things you can't change so shouldn't worry about. One is the past, and the other is the weather. Ypsilanti didn't miss out on the summer heat wave, and it was unpleasantly hot. The evenings were a treat though, and we loved being outside, usually enjoying a BBQ and watching the fireflies twirling and flitting about. None of us Kiwis had ever seen these before and were captivated by them. We also spent our evenings putting the covers (slicks) into the transparent sleeves of the DVD cases. This was not quite a competitive sport, but it nearly became one. It was all done mob-handed with great spirit and not a little beer. Later it transpired that our quality assurance wasn't great, and more than one person bought a product with no DVD inside ... oops.

Sandy and Pat had a nice middle-class suburban home in a leafy suburb with wide streets, nice lawns and no front fences. They had a double garage for the requisite toys (motorbike) and a large covered trailer that held our books and DVDs as well as more toys (another motorbike for Pat and a little bike for the grandkids), and in the neighbour's drive they had the motor-home parked up. There was a sizeable backyard with a shed and good space for the grandkids to play. As with most American homes, they had a basement where the central heating boiler and laundry lived, and this was also a workshop and storage area containing all the gadgetry and products that places like Walmart foist on their customers. On one hand, they had so much that many would envy them, yet on the other, they were typical of the middle-class almost-poor of America. Life is a struggle, – not like the real poor of the ghetto and slum areas but still a struggle. One morning while passively sharing Myles's early morning smoke, I passed the comment, "for simple folks, there is no simplicity in their lives." This wasn't meant as a criticism but just an observation. Only a year earlier, I'd been sharing Mongolian gers with folk who were also just simple working-class Joes. Their lives were no better, no worse ... just simpler.

We'd been awed by the contents of the motor-home shop with its gadgets for everything. All of them were 'labour-saving', but I felt that you'd end up with a storage unit filled with them and any time saved would have been spent on finding the right one, working out how it worked, did it still work, doing the bizzo, cleaning it and putting it away again. Pat had a good number of them, but he still had a long way to go. Every time we went in the shop, we'd take the opportunity to sit in the vibrating chair on display and whinny with delight. I think it was an after-market driver's seat.

Many Americans seem to go for quantity rather than quality, and often when we'd ask Pat about something that to us looked like a frenzy of consumerism, he'd reply simply, "It's the American way." Myles was also overwhelmed by the number of TV sets and the way they were used as pacifiers for the kids. From his TV-free world, it was alien to him but we both know that there is no 'right' way to bring up children, just different ways. We laughed also at the frequent shouts of "Shut the door, the cats will get out!" We were more familiar with the reverse of this, where you put the cats out and shut doors to keep them out. I remember with amusement on our honeymoon staying up at the family homestead where my mother grew up, and my gentle aunt kept scooping up cats and apparently putting them in a cupboard. Every time a cousin came in the door, a couple more cats would come in, and sooner or later Aunt Zita would capture them and fling them into the cupboard. Steph confessed later to being amazed that this gentle woman could be so coolly and casually piling these poor felines into the cupboard. She'd seen at least 12 go in and thought it must be a bigger cupboard than it looked or they must be very squashed. Of course, I had knew it was the woodbox with access to the outside and knew that the cats were constantly being recycled.

A couple of things were becoming apparent. One was that the Honda was not quite going to be ready to ride off to Mid-Ohio, so our trip there would have to be a 'there and back' one and we'd not be carrying on around the bottom of Lake Erie and into Canada through Buffalo. This just meant a minor change, and we'd alter the route to ride directly through Detroit to Toronto. As long as there were no more delays, everything would still fit. There were other logistical problems beginning to surface. Pat wouldn't go to Canada. He wouldn't say why, just that he and Canada didn't get on. There were also a couple of states that the same was said of, and the reasons for it remained a mystery to us. Usually the conversation went something like "xxx and me don't get along – I went there once". The other thing was that Sandy really wasn't so keen on having a bottle of helium transported around in their motor-home. Pat was also less than enthusiastic about it and gave us numerous technical reasons why it was dangerous. Pat was good at not making an issue about it, and Sandy had never directly said no … but we already felt we were not helping the stressful time she was going through. It also wasn't fair that Pat should be the meat in the sandwich. He shouldn't even be anywhere near the sandwich.

We decided that the solution would be to hire a van ourselves for the weekend and take it down to Mid-Ohio with the helium and all our stuff in it, then return for the bikes and depart on the Monday. Even this wasn't simple, as several hire places were fully booked and others wouldn't let us go interstate. Pat got onboard with all this and ferried us around until we found Mel's Auto Services who had a Rent-A-Wreck franchise. Part of the enjoyment of travelling is the interplay with strangers who intersect your life ever so briefly. For us, the simple hiring of a van provided us with one of those interludes. The woman behind the counter was one of those characters you remember with fondness all your life. Of early middle age, middle height and sturdy … but not overly so, she had short curly blonde hair, a square face, heavily made-up eyes, a tattoo on her inner forearm near the elbow, fingernails almost an inch long and the manner and backchat that only a lifetime of dealing with the rough-and-ready could have given her. She may never have been super-attractive, even in her youth, but she still oozed appeal and character. She had a face that seemed made of India-rubber, and her way of making an eyebrow rise without otherwise moving made us laugh constantly. Initially, she declined our request as being outside a 200 mile radius. Mel himself then passed through the room, and without hesitation he said OK. About then, she spotted Kitty filming and asked, "What's with the camera?" Upon being told that we were from New Zealand and were making a documentary and after Myles's comment that she looked worried, she raised an eyebrow and said, "That's OK then, all my warrants are paid!" She gave us the usual complex equation of so much a day, so much for insurance and so much per mile. Myles then asked for a bit of paper or a calculator. Without comment, she pushed in front of him a calculator with a blank digital screen. Hesitantly, while familiarising himself with its layout, Myles responded that it was a bit technical. "Plus is for more and minus is for less," she drolly quipped back with forbearance. Ultimately, she came up with a figure of $60 per day including 100 miles allocation, insurance and damage waiver. "You're our person," said Myles. Coyly she responded, "That's been said before." Her repartee was always immediate and pointed.

As she filled out the paperwork, Mel passed back through the room and, hearing that we were from New Zealand, posed the question, "What part?" For 30 years, I have waited for this opportunity. "All of me!" I replied. I must admit it's not original, having seen a Kev the Kiwi cartoon in London in the 1970s where the same answer was given. It scored a good laugh here though and evened out the interchanges a little. They gave us cookies and coffee, and all went well until we were taking our leave saying we'd be back in the morning to pick up the van. Our femme raised one eyebrow a full 2 inches and expressed ire. "So why have I done all this paperwork now?" she growled. We didn't know whether to be scared or not. We asked her to raise the eyebrow again for the camera, telling her that it was scary. "It's meant to be," she drawled.

Wednesday night turned out to be almost disastrous and certainly was stressful for me. Early evening, I realised that my wallet was missing. We all know this feeling … there's a small knot of fear passes deeply across your belly. Questioningly, you doubt for a moment then bravely affirm that you are sure it will turn up. But no, Pat's van was searched, my room was searched, I was searched, the house was searched, Shauna was rung at a nightclub … just in case she had taken it by mistake, the local store was revisited, the deserted Police station was visited, every possibility was investigated. Ultimately we admitted it was not going to be found so I had to ring the Visa card people and put a stop to my card. In the middle of this drama, Dennis from Dearborn arrived. He was the friend and agent of the woman who had sold me the BMW, and we'd connected well during the process. He'd driven quite a way to catch up with us, and all he got was me in a tizz. He has also been the person who almost got us the sales opportunity with Ford. We liked what little we saw of him. I knew he had a Studebaker hidden away interstate somewhere, and I know he'd have loved to talk about Dick's one, which he had seen in the copy I'd sent him of the 5 minute TV interview that had been screened on national television in New Zealand. I hoped that this wouldn't be the last contact with him. I knew I would like him, given the chance. Fortunately, Myles eased him aside and chatted while I continued to run around like a headless chook. A couple of international calls had cancelled my card and given me instructions on how to replace it.

The night had been ruined, Dennis went home, I hoped not fuming at travelling the 20 miles or so for the abortive visit. I was a little gloomy and disappointed in myself. For whatever reason, I had not yet established an away-from-home personal routine. I didn't know it, but it would get worse before it got better. Quite late we started the process of retiring to bed. Suddenly, a shriek rent the air. Sandra had found the wallet lying under a little plastic booster stool that stood in front of the toilet for the small ones to stand on. It was completely hidden from sight if standing … however, when seated on the throne, it could be glimpsed. Thank heavens for the difference of the sexes and their toilet practices. It was too late to uncancel the card but it was great to have my wallet back with everything else it contained. A much more relaxed sleep followed.

The day before at Mel's, when asking how early we could pick up the van, they had replied that when we got up they'd be there already. We could have the van at 7.00 am. "I get up at 5.30," said Myles, "but he gets up at 11.30," nodding at Pat. "I can be here at 7.00," insisted Pat, and so an early start was cast in stone. We'd really wanted to leave at lunchtime so it was a rush sorting out a temporary Visa card, collecting the helium bottle and loading up the van. Pat had decided he wanted to go to the track for the weekend in his motor-home, which still wasn't quite fully prepared. Mid-afternoon saw a decision taken that Kitty and I would head off in the van while Myles would wait and keep Pat company in the motor-home when it was ready. This was a generous act as I know Myles was just as eager as Kitty and me to hit the road. It was just a small gesture of loyalty to Pat who had selflessly been at Myles's beck and call for the last 10 days or so, and who had earlier followed lots of my obscure instructions by email to the best of his ability ... even paying for some items for me when vendors needed local monies. It looked like they would be another one to two hours, and we were eager to go and get established before dark.

And so it was, with a light head and a hopeful heart, that I made my way out onto the North American highway system. The interstate highways have a simple and logical layout. The one and two-digit roads are the normal highways arranged so the even numbers are east-west routes and the odd numbers are north-south routes. When there is a three-digit sign, if the first digit is even, it means that it is a route through or around a city. If the first number is odd, however, it means that it is a spur road into a city and it doesn't go through it. So when you are travelling interstate you don't take a three-digit highway beginning with an odd number as it will leave you in a town and not take you out the other side. So armed with a map and a navigator, not a lot could go wrong ... and it didn't. By dusk, we'd found our 20 foot by 20 foot plot that would be our home for the next 3 days. We decided that there was room for us to put the 'selling' gazebo along the front, and we'd put up our little tents behind where the site backed onto a big access road and we would camp onsite.

Myles and Pat were a couple of hours behind, but ultimately found us, and Pat even managed to get the motor-home parked on the wide verge on the other side of the access road. It was an ideal set-up. Although Pat was keen for us to use his air-conditioned luxury, we were keener to be in our own little tents. Kitty did take up his invitation. Whether it was to get away from me or a selfless act of demonstrating appreciation towards Pat, I don't know. She had enjoyed his music and crazy talk. We were chalk and cheese really, and I don't think Pat could understand us Kiwis and our urgent and sometimes strange ways.

The Vintage Days were … well, I wrote this at the time:

The AMA Vintage Days at Mid-Ohio are an institution for old-bike fans. Not only are there three days of all sorts of classic racing for the action enthusiasts, but there are retailers offering specials and 1,000 stalls in the swap meet area. Being in America and run by the AMA means that it is well organised and very professional. This year featured MV Augusta and Hodaka as the specialty marques. There were huge numbers of both in evidence. The three days are well planned with something happening at all times. In addition to the racing and the swap meet [or auto jumble as the English would call it], there were seminars every hour or so by notable people on all sorts of topics. Stunt riders entertained at times, as did some Police display teams. There was also a rock band that had a few spots, and as always with this type of event, there were the riders' bikes. Someone told me that 100,000 attend over the three days, and I am not in a position to disagree. Every type of bike imaginable was represented there. There were the huge cruisers towing trailers as would be expected, but also

there were hundreds of mini-bikes for running around on. The Honda 70 Trail of the 1970s would have been the most popular for riding around the swap meet (after golf carts, which are hired for this purpose – everything is

just so big and spread out). Many beautifully restored examples of the 70s were drooled over by Myles, as he has had one since his youth. He dutifully bought a few parts for his and photographed one from every angle for later.

The crowds were huge in more ways than one, and never have I seen so many inappropriately clad (unclad) and displayed menfolk's bodies. It was hot on all days which encouraged the masses to dispense with their shirts. Huge bellies overhung everywhere you looked. I have never seen so many obese people in one place (I only see one image in the bathroom mirror, and it is mostly fogged up). It was fascinating even though a bit repulsive … I'll never be reticent about taking my shirt off in public again … well not in America. Many of the bodies should be donated to medical science for research purposes. Not all were middle-aged either, and one young guy fascinated me as he had the most unfortunate body shape … yet proudly displayed himself every day as he walked around with his pretty, petite blonde girlfriend. He was tall, thinnish and soft looking, with a very narrow hairless chest, planted on which were two pert conical breasts (like Madonna's bra), and below this was an impressive paunch. Good on him, you say, as he was obviously happy with his space … and you are right, but I am not removing my tee-shirt until I am 85 kg.

Some of the tee-shirts were great though, and one being worn by a massive fat guy proudly said 'I survived anorexia'.

Although every type of bike was in evidence from old American, Russian, Czech, Danish (Nimbus), German, British, Italian, Spanish, Canadian etc., by far the biggest in numbers were the early Japanese. There were numerous Bridgestone 350s, YDS2 and YDS3 Yamahas, all the early Honda Dreams, Super Hawks etc. Another well-presented group was the Penton riders who even had an old Penton posed climbing over a tree stump. Lots of exotica was for sale, and what took my fancy was an early 50s NSU 350 in original condition. Numerous Ducati singles also seemed to be for sale, and very nice many of them looked too.

We had a tent displaying the Last Hurrah stuff, and while we didn't become instant millionaires, we sold books and DVDs steadily on all days. We had our promotional weather balloon flying above the tent for two of the days, but just like kids' party balloons … it popped. We camped alongside our display, as did a few others. We made quite a number of friends and as always had a few laughs. It had been fascinating for us and a little disappointing that we hadn't really been able to fully sample what Mid-Ohio had to offer. We were just too busy. I did get to watch the old master Agostini howl around the circuit, neat and tidy as you'd expect of one with over 120 GP victories. My biggest memories are of the massive scale of the event and the well-trained efficient workers. There were clean toilets, quite good showers and heaps to look at. Impressive also was how the swap meet punters often had little hand carts to carry away their Triumph 650 crankshafts or their CZ engines. Some entrepreneurs even had them for hire ... smart, eh!

But a lot more happened at Mid-Ohio. There was the good – we met

ZEN AND THE LAST HURRAH

46

with Del Smylie, the AMA Chairman (selling him a book and DVD), we were interviewed by the TV crew putting together the promo for next year, we met Mary and Lee Cowie of Motorsport Publications who are Panther Publishing's representatives in North America, we met Buzz and Pixie Walneck of Classic Cycle Trader ... and numerous other trade connections. But the not so good was that I wasn't made rich and famous overnight, and the reality of the ongoing trip had to be faced. Both the Cowies and the Walnecks take their enterprises to numerous similar events across the US each year, but neither would contemplate going to Sturgis to trade. "Hell, it's the Budweiser Nationals!" we were told. "You go there to drink and get a tattoo, not buy a book." This thought had been brewing for a little while, and without a progression of movie screenings etc. arranged for along the way, the realisation was sinking in that *The Last Hurrah* was not going to fly. Hard decisions had to be faced up to. It was hard, as a lot of effort had gone into getting the books and DVDs to the US in time for this trip. It had to be admitted that my promotion had been woeful, and if we brought Pat along across the US carting all our gear in the behemoth, then paid for him to go back to Ypsilanti, I'd be ruined. The motor-home only did about 5 miles to the gallon, and fuel prices were already climbing. The saving on accommodation costs would only be minimal as we'd be camping a lot of the time, so economically it just didn't stack up. But what to do with all the gear and the stock? My mood sank with the misty evening rain. Would the sun shine again tomorrow?

Into the picture strode Richard Backus. Lean and lanky with a strong voice and an easy laugh. "It's serendipity," he insisted. He and his sidekick Andrew were the driving force behind a new glossy magazine called *Motorcycle Classics*. With only the least amount of coaxing, they would take our stock, gazebo and all. They had a big articulated truck that had a workshop with five or six bikes in it at the back, and sumptuous living quarters made up the rest. The outsides were vividly emblazoned with their logo and advertising. Primarily black, this rig was like something out of a Hollywood movie. Apparently, their principals had given them two years to 'go for it'. They were to make the profile of the magazine by being everywhere, with an 'in your face' presence. In addition to getting me out of the poo, they would sell the stock through their magazine shop, so it looked like a classic win/win. Lee and Mary also took a bit of our stock and the left-overs from the other Panther Publishing books that Rollo had sent over, but the main lot was lugged down to the big, black truck and stored away.

It wasn't one of my best performances as I told Pat the news that his motor-home wouldn't be our mobile hotel and packhorse for the next while ... not even down to Sturgis. I don't do these sorts of things well. I could sense Pat's disappointment, and I knew that, back at home, Sandy would also be disappointed as they were looking forward to what they call camping. Once the decision had been made, quite a load came off my shoulders. Myles and Kitty were supportive and had really helped me make the decision. Sometimes you just have to look ahead and cut your losses, then move on. We'd had fun, worked hard and now we were going to start the real adventure afresh. *The Last Hurrah* was dead, the *Zen* ride about to begin. It would give us a new and relaxed focus ... not needing to worry about success. But somewhere in this dithering, confused part of the weekend, I lost my wallet again. I didn't realise until going to buy petrol in the neighbouring town ... bugger! How unbelievably stupid, how inept and incompetent! I could remember having it at the *Motorcycle Classics* truck, so back we went as fast as we could, but no, it was gone. I retraced my footsteps everywhere I had been, knowing what a fool I would appear having to cancel my new Visa card. Would they believe that it wasn't some sort of obscure scam? By now, it was the time that everyone was packing up and leaving. Myles and Pat had already left, so I was spared that humiliation but missed the extra eyes.

Again, in a darkish mood, we made our way along the couple of miles of internal road to the exit. Near the exit was another 'command post,' which we decided was worth a crack in the forlorn hope that someone had handed in the wallet ... yep! Wooo hooo ... it was there! These 'pretend' set-backs seemed to be a warning. "Get your act together, boy!" someone seemed to be saying. I don't know why I was so obviously disorganised – I just didn't have a routine. From that moment, I have been rigid in my habits. Wallet goes in zipped right pocket, Swiss Army knife goes in left pocket, hanky in each. If only I could have been spared the embarrassment by doing this earlier. Character-building stuff it may be, but I blush at the memory.

Kitty and I didn't quite make an immaculate return, straight as an arrow – no, for a while, we did seem to be temporarily misplaced on the planet. We ended up wandering through a poor suburb, not all that far from where we wanted to go to, but worlds' away in the reality of life. We didn't see any white faces, and we were yelled at a couple of times. We couldn't make out what was said, but it didn't seem to indicate that they'd like to invite a couple of weary travellers in for a cup of tea. Racism is something I don't understand because it isn't rational, but sadly it is real. For some reason, we don't seem to like people who are different from us. Sometimes this is just a colour thing, sometimes it is a religious thing, sometimes it is a national thing and sometimes it is just a sports club thing. The authorities in the UK go to great lengths to keep the various hard-core soccer followers apart each week. Sometimes trouble happens when the teams aren't even playing each other. Once there was even an instance of two 'soccer express' trains that were travelling to different parts of the country. Sadly, the trains had occasion to stop opposite each other. The fans attacked each other and left at least one dead from stab wounds. They hated each other for no reason other than they were fans of another team. I remember shifting to a small provincial town in New Zealand and in conversation with a nice neighbour of Dutch extraction, being told that he "didn't mind the Māoris (he'd grown up with lots of them) but he didn't like the (Pacific) Islanders". I replied with surprise that I didn't realise there were many in the region. It turned out that he'd never met one but was quite happy to spread his racial vitriol. Having travelled to about 50 countries, I know that deep down we're all very, very similar, and I feel sorrow every time I hear of an experience of racial intolerance.

The plan was becoming clearer. We would head directly across through Detroit to Mississauga on the outskirts of Toronto where Steph's uncle Brian and aunt Gwyneth live. We could then 'do' Niagara Falls as a day trip before heading off up over the top of Lake Huron before re-entering the US at Sault Ste Marie and making our way down to St Paul to start the *Zen* ride. There were still lots of things to do, so on Monday morning, Myles had us up at 10 to five (which is just after midnight), and we beavered away tying up all the last loose ends to get Myles's Honda through the processes with the Secretary of State so we could have at least some semblance of being legal. We knew that we would struggle to go through international borders if we weren't pretty squeaky clean. As is often the case, we were trying to bite off more than we could chew, and by lunchtime, we had realised it wasn't sensible to try and head off for Canada that day. So we fully packed the bikes and left them outside on the back lawn, all ready for an early start on Tuesday morning. Pat had donated all sorts of things to the cause including a magnetic tank bag for the Honda. It was a relief to find that we could pack almost everything we wanted to take with us. A few things were left (mainly Kitty's), and Pat arranged for them to be sent on later. Stage one was complete. We'd stuttered, we'd stammered, we'd hiccupped but we'd succeeded ... so far.

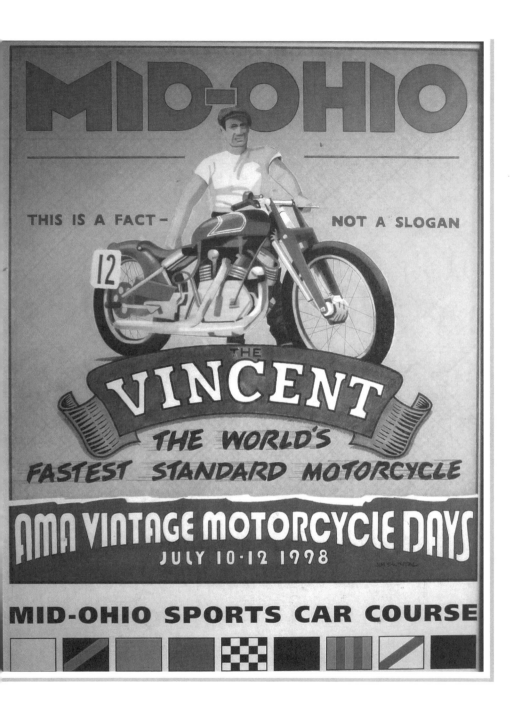

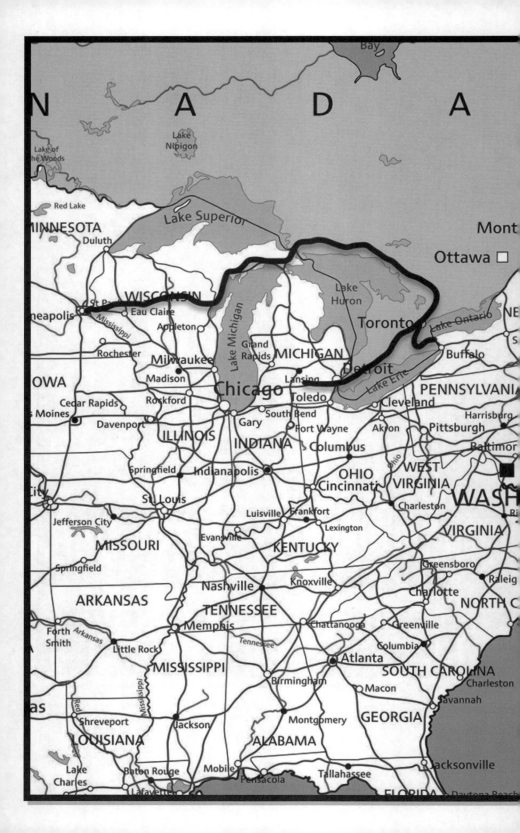

Chapter Three

UNLEASHED

I'm always excited on beginning a motorcycle adventure because it combines two wonderful things, and it promises ... well, you don't really know what it promises ... what will be, will be, and that is part of the appeal. Motorcycling is an addiction that, for those of us so afflicted, we are hopeful they'll never find a cure for. To try and describe the freedom and enjoyment of motorcycling has challenged even the most erudite. My own attempts usually involve a lot of arm waving and exaggerated superlatives. The unconverted have no idea of the quantum leap that is taken when the tin-top box is exchanged for a freedom machine. I remember riding the Andes in my youth with towering peaks leaning over me, filling me with awe, as I could also look down thousands of feet into valleys far below, blurring the details with distance. I could feel the scale of the mountains, I could smell the countryside, I could sense the enormity of the slopes seeming to rush away to infinity below. A few days later, I had occasion to make a bus trip along the same road to Quito in Ecuador. My views were now framed and constrained. There was no sense of being in the picture; I was a spectator, not a participant. It was pale and puny, barely worth remembering, not something I would recall with clarity 30 years later.

Pirsig puts it quite well:

You see things vacationing on a motorcycle in a way that is completely different from any other. In a car you're always in a compartment, and because you're used to it you don't realize that through that car window everything is more TV. You're a passive observer and it is all moving by you boringly in a frame. On a cycle the frame is gone. You're completely in contact with it all. You're in the scene, not just watching it anymore, and the sense of presence is over-whelming. That concrete whizzing by 5 inches below your foot is the real thing, the same stuff you walk on, it's right there, so blurred you can't focus on it, yet you can put your foot down and touch it anytime, and the whole experience is never removed from immediate consciousness.

The other thing about a motorcycle is that, just like riding a horse, you control it in so many small ways. You put the bike exactly where you want it in a corner by a series of tiny manoeuvres of your body. The moving of a buttock, a knee put out, a dropped shoulder, a weight transfer from one foot peg to another, a twitch of the throttle hand all affect where and how the bike tracks. It is your individual skill that does it. You counter-steer by pushing your right bar away to turn right quickly. The bike starts to fall to the right, and without realising it, you catch it with a reactive adjustment and together you glide and swish around bends. It is like ballet with a machine. With competence gained, it feels so good. It is an extension of your body, not a vehicle to be guided by remote controls of steering through a transfer box of worm gear and racks, pinions and the like. You think through bends, and the motorcycle listens to those thoughts and movements. The process is so precise and balanced that, if as a male you dress to the left, you carry your Swiss Army knife in your right pocket. Victorinox even make their knives in different sizes to enable this delicate balancing of the ballasts. Your requirement might call for a little Pocket Pal or anything up to the impressive Swiss Champ. Combining the physical enjoyment of taming this wondrous steed with the sensory experience of the environment traps you for life. Enjoy.

And then you add in adventure! For me, adventure is leaving behind the constraints of the repetitiousness of our everyday life. Some people think that adventures are only done by adventurers, which is so sad and inaccurate. Adventurers tend to be elite athletes who drag husky dogs across frozen wastelands (snacking on them when hungry) or row tiny boats across large, open oceans. But reflect ... life is an adventure. Watch children as they discover in life, they rush to the next stage, corner, hill, whatever, with excitement and eagerness ... because they have never been there. They run ahead because they want to find out what is around that next corner. Sadly, we seem to lose that eagerness and thrill as we mature into the plateau that is so often our 'grown-up' state ... and then it is time to ease up and prepare for our own demise and transfer to the next world. To end the short *Last Hurrah* TV interview done in New Zealand, we had made a couple of off-the-cuff statements that, on reflection, I was quite proud of, with many people ringing me to say how much they agreed with the sentiments. First Dick said, "Don't wait too long, or before you know it, you're knackered." This was particularly poignant, because the watching public didn't know that interview had been delayed for a couple of weeks while Dick recovered from a stroke. The wonderful closing shot showed Dick and me riding away on a very dusty, rough mountain road, and the camera slowly widened out the shot to show the enormity of the Karakoram mountains that we were heading into accompanied by my voice-over: "We're not adventurers but we're having a hellava adventure. You don't have to be Tim Severin or Bonnington or Hillary to have an adventure. Your adventure is what you do."

So for the most wonderful experience, you put together motorcycles and adventure. Take it away Steppenwolf! "Get your motor running, head out on the highwaaayyy!" And so it was we said fond farewells, and headed off into and through Detroit. No time for decent shake-down rides, we were desperate to end the apparent inactivity and ride, ride, ride. It may have been rush-hour traffic but we didn't care. We settled on a steady 60 mph as feeling good for both bikes. No matter where I went, no matter how erratic my lane changing was, Myles stuck to my tail. This was part fear, part skill. We don't run to intercoms or the like, and Kitty and I communicated by yelling and prodding, pointing and shaking. Myles communicated by sticking in the mirrors, occasionally riding alongside to indicate fuel or food need.

This first day on the road had no real highlights other than the initial euphoria of successfully leaving the US. The ride to the border was exciting because it was the first ride fully laden and out of range of home base. The border crossing was achieved with no real dramas, and our paperwork seemed to pass muster, allowing us to ride up over the big Ambassador Bridge crossing the Detroit River, which links the huge lakes Erie and Huron. The bridge is the single busiest international land border crossing in North America and consequently was quite impressive in operation. It made the 4–5 hour border crossings of Central Asia look really sick. The bridge is more than 1.5 miles long from tollbooth to inspection checkpoint and operates 24 hours a day, 7 days a week. And so into Windsor and Canada. It was novel being back in a 'British' country, and we were surprised to find signs in kilometres rather than miles. We learned later that the temperatures were given in Celsius, just as we were used to at home. A mid-morning stop at an archetypal roadside diner promised much but delivered disappointingly little. It looked like the staple of North American culture, but in reality was so average – the first of many. We did encounter a motorcycle couple there, which was more enjoyable than the diner experience. They were middle-aged and had a huge deep-plum-coloured Harley Davidson clone (Kawasaki?) with tassels hanging from the handlebars, a big windscreen and leg-shields, three headlights, a scalloped, capacious twin-level seat with a backrest for the pillion, enormous luggage boxes and twin aerials reaching skywards at the back – presumably to power the radios, intercoms etc. They were just taking a day off and enjoying a short ride to do breakfast. Our bikes looked so small and puny in comparison, but as they say, "it is

ZEN AND THE LAST HURRAH
58

not the size of dog in the fight, but the size of the fight in the dog."

There was nothing much in the ride to Mississuaga to enjoy. The countryside was low and flat with little choice of road. The roads we did travel on were filled with trucks carrying freight to or from the US border we'd just passed over. More than $100 billion of trade crosses that Ambassador Bridge every year. It was a long and wearying 400 kilometre day before we finally reached the welcoming haven of Brian and Gwyn Stewart's cosy little home. Brian was Steph's mum's youngest brother, who in the late 1950s had met and married a young Welsh woman in New Zealand before travelling to Canada. After a long and distinguished career with Canadian Broadcasting, Brian was now retired and enjoying his golf. A brush with cancer was only just behind him. (Sadly it would return and claim his life in 2007.) I'd met Brian several times on his visits back to see his siblings and to renew his Kiwi roots. He was amusingly gentle and, I suspect, a gentleman. For one who knew so much from a life of journalism, he never pushed himself or his points of view to the fore. He always listened more than he talked. I'd not met Gwyn, as she had not been back to New Zealand for many years.

Steph had stayed with them when she lived in the US for a period in the 1970s before I met her, and son Stephen had called in to visit when on his way to Europe. "She's lovely," was always Steph's description. Small and quiet, yes she was, and still is lovely. A person who you just like. You don't have to get to know her to like her … it just happens. The bikes were secured in their garage, and we reviewed their performance so far. Myles wanted a day just tinkering and tweaking, and while he did that, Kitty and I would explore Toronto, then we'd ride down to Niagara the next day before riding up through Toronto and up out into the semi-wilderness beyond. Brian's good neighbour Kevin would ride with us to Niagara on his 1972 Triumph Bonneville. Kevin had followed *The Last Hurrah* and was interested in our project. He'd tried to get his club organised to have a promo night with them, but they weren't keen to move their club night, so nothing eventuated. I left some books and DVDs with him to distribute.

It had become evident as I neared Mississauga that my BMW would need a small job done on it that made me smile. The mirror clamp was not holding the mirror on to the handlebars firmly enough, and the wind pressure at speed was causing it to slip around. Even fully tightened it was slipping. This delighted me because something very similar caused dissension in the Pirsig camp, and this had been highlighted to me by a young friend Leon back in New Zealand just before I left. "Don't forget the Coke can," he jibed. Pirsig's travelling companion John Sutherland, the BMW owner, had a real phobia about mechanical things, preferring to know nothing about the problems or their solutions. Pirsig tried to interest him in mechanical things, but he resisted strongly and almost irrationally. He appeared to have no mechanical feel, which meant that at times he had problems even starting the bike, although it was new. He flooded the bike one time by using the choke when the bike didn't need it. He thought that 'use full choke when cold' meant that, every time the engine was stopped, it should be used to restart. When admonished by Pirsig, who explained that the engine was still warm as they'd only been away 30 minutes and it was a hot day, he'd snapped, "Well, why don't they tell you that in the instructions?" Another time, it happened again that the bike was reluctant to fire into life, but rather than interfere with a suggestion, Pirsig watched as the Sutherlands took 15 minutes to get the bike running. Later John whined:

"They just had this one motorcycle, see? This lemon. And they didn't know what to do with it, whether to send it back to the factory, or sell it for scrap or what … and then at the last moment, they saw me coming. With eighteen hundred bucks in my pocket. And they knew their problems were over."

Eighteen hundred dollars would have almost bought three Honda Super

Hawks like Pirsig's. The BMW was the epitome of a 'gentleman's express' — exclusive, quiet, sophisticated and reliable.

Part-way through the *Zen* ride, Sutherland found that the handlebars were just slipping a little and couldn't be tightened enough to grip fully. Pirsig tells him:

"You're going to have to shim those out,"

"What's shim?"

"It's a thin, flat strip of metal. You just slip it around the handlebar under the collar there and it will open up the collar to where you can tighten it again. You use shims like that to make adjustments in all kinds of machines."

"Oh," Sutherland said, getting interested. "Good. Where do you buy them?"

"I've some right here," said Pirsig gleefully holding up a can of beer in his hand. Initially Sutherland didn't understand, then said "What, the can?"

"Sure" said Pirsig "best shim stock in the world."

Pirsig had thought it pretty clever, but to his amazement, Sutherland was offended that he had the nerve to propose to repair his new $1,800 BMW, the pride of a half-century of German mechanical finesse, with a piece of old beer can. It didn't get repaired.

For us, this was great, the present mirroring the past. We didn't quite get it right as my mind told me it was a Coke can and I didn't reread the passage to check and learn that it was a beer can, but it matters not at all. With Kitty filming, we cut a strip of shim material and wrapped it around the handlebars and subsequently did up the clamp which, tightened without 'bottoming'. Very successful, something Sutherland should have allowed happen in 1968. As Pirsig recorded:

… beer-can aluminium is soft and sticky as metals go. Perfect for the application. Aluminium doesn't oxidize in wet weather-or, more precisely it always has a thin layer of oxide that prevents any further oxidation. Also perfect. In other words, any true German mechanic, with a half-century of

mechanical finesse behind him, would have concluded that this particular
solution to this particular technical problem was perfect.

I think Kitty was relieved to be filming something that she felt had some relevance. She had on occasion asked, "What if nothing happens?" I think she felt we needed to have something dramatic happen like a bike crash or something to make her filming have a power. I think also that she felt she needed to match Stephen's effort with *The Last Hurrah* when he recorded unexpected but necessary hospital visits in Mongolia, Kyrgyzstan, China and Iran, a broken front fork-leg repair in Pakistan and the evacuation of Dick from Southern Iran. Personally, I wanted none of those reruns or anything similar. She hadn't been able to film any huge triumph at Mid-Ohio, but she'd captured the mood and scale of the event. There was no despondency lingering.

After a nice night catching up with family gossip, Kitty and I headed off by train into the metropolis that is Toronto. Armed with my GPS, we set off for a day of exploration and hopefully fun in a city that contains more than the population of New Zealand. It was good to be out doing something one on one with Kitty, because with four children, it is rare that this happens. I hoped our five weeks together would be memorable for the bond it should engender. As a way of further hoping to share a little of her world, I had agreed to be a vegetarian for the period together. I told myself that it was only five weeks of my life and it would add a challenge to the adventure. So far, it had been not too hard because Sandy and Shauna were good (and familiar) with vegetarian meals. Kitty and Myles had enjoyed the nature of having a home base for a week and a half, and they too created nice repasts. On the road would be a different proposition. I felt that, here in the home of big meat-eaters, I would struggle and was prepared to always be envious of Myles's meals, presuming that I would be eating something far less appealing, probably green and grass-like.

The first thing that struck me with Toronto was the people. They weren't as big and fat as Americans ... I kid you not, once over the bridge, the level of obesity definitely dropped. That is not to say there weren't big Canadians, but the numbers were down. I started to count how many fat people per city block, and sometimes I would find none. That would never have happened in Detroit, Ypsilanti, Ann Arbor etc. The Western world is in the grips of an obesity epidemic, which I had also observed in Europe in 2005. New Zealand is not missing in this, but we do pale in comparison. Being so pertinent, I wondered how the US Military found enough troops to send off on active duty. Judging by what I'd seen, it would have to be mainly inactive duty. I've heard the term 'desensitised' used in relation to what we in the modern world are exposed to. They say (ever wondered who 'they' are?) that, by being exposed by TV to atrocities and natural disasters so often, we have become desensitised and don't find these things shocking anymore. They just become ho hum and almost ordinary. I felt that was the scenario that fitted what I had seen at Mid-Ohio. Take one obese young person, and stripping off his top in most places would bring 'shock, horror, yuck'. In the US, it seems people have been exposed to so many obese bodies that it has become quite acceptable and normal and only shocking to outsiders. Those who know me are probably shaking their heads and muttering about the pot calling the kettle black ... but it is sad when you follow a fattie-mum filling her supermarket trolley with doughnuts and cookies etc., being followed around by her fattie-kids. Fattie-dad was probably waiting in the car.

The buildings of Toronto were often modern and quite striking. I photographed many for later use in a building publication I write for. I was hopeful some would be used in the 'Spot the changes' competition. They were the right sorts of buildings for that. There was something else that was strikingly different – something so obvious that it took me a little while to figure it out. Being on the same land mass and speaking often with a similar accent (to our ears), I had always thought of Canadians as 'almost Americans' and things would be very similar. But no, quite different. What was missing were the flags, the patriotic flags that adorn every lamp post and building in most US cities. We'd seen flags that were many, many storeys high. Cars and motorbikes flying flags are as common as fat people. Often the two are combined. Here, there wasn't the overt almost-feverish, patriotism on display. Somehow, that was reassuring. In New Zealand, we also don't do big flag displays. While in Canada, do what the Canadians do ... and I did. I bought a pair of Crocs – the plastic clogs with holes in the toes. We also walked and walked, and talked and walked, then followed the GPS's magic arrow back to the train station. It was a couple of tired little pixies who returned home that night

Kevin took me out that night to a carpark display of bikes and cars. In the summer, on each Wednesday night, an informal motoring get-together takes place where you bring and show, yarn with your mates and generally have some fun. There were some drastically modified cars and numerous choppers gleaming in the halflight. This was relaxed and fun. Music played, and the young strutted and strolled. Those with tattoos wore sleeveless muscle tees to show off their pretty pictures. The techno-bores mumbled about triple chrome, hemi heads, forward controls, OCC wheels, razor-cut front ends etc. All this was pretty cool, with a lot of money invested in these leisure vehicles. None of them looked like they'd be up for a cross-country adventure though. We were only three-quarters around ... second time mind, as initially I skimmed like a kid in a candy store, first looking at the shiny and glitzy, the sort of stuff you don't see in real life ... when suddenly there was an announcement over the PA that there was a storm front closing fast and there would be rain in 15 minutes. Hell, that got them going! It was like a confused Le Mans start to a motor race where, when the flag drops, you run to your car or motorbike, jump in or on, start it as quickly as you can and race off down the track. This time, they ran from all over the place, and with a hell of a lot of horsepower making a hell of a lot of noise, they went off in all sorts of directions with as much speed and style as they could muster. There is a saying that "chrome don't get you home", but I reckon this time it did, as all these rufty-tufties weren't going to let any precipitation reach the copper-nickel-chrome plating they had invested thousands of dollars in. It did mean that the evening was slightly truncated and an earlier night eventuated than what might have been expected.

We farewelled Brian early next morning before he went off for an early morning game of golf, then breakfasted with Gwyn, watching with fascination a cheeky squirrel playing in her garden. It came running and skipping along the garden wall and leapt out onto a tree branch. We have no members of the Sciuridae family (squirrels, chipmunks, marmots, prairie dogs and woodchucks) in New Zealand, and they never fail to fascinate when seen up close. Gwyn said she knows they are a pest, but she is only half-hearted in her efforts to keep them away, as she too thinks they are quite cute. Kitty then took the pillion seat behind Kevin, and they led the way off to Niagara with Myles and me roaming alongside from time to time for filming. Later she told us she was getting electric shocks from his bike every time she put her hands on anything metal … which made it a bit interesting to try and hold on. The ride to Niagara was only 100 miles, and we were there by mid-morning. Niagara was as spectacular as expected, and we enjoyed the experience of being at one of the world's greatest natural wonders. I smiled at the sight of the tumbling waters and the spray clouds, and from the view points at the upper levels we could watch the funny, old-fashioned stubby little round-ended two-storey ferry boats seeming to challenge the power of the roaring falls as they ducked into the misty clouds, way below us. I mainly was smiling because 30 years earlier when Steph visited this wondrous example of nature, it was turned off for cleaning or some such. It was hard to credit, but she swears it is true.

The ride back to Toronto was dull and cool, moving towards cold and even wet enough to make us stop and tog up. The ride through Toronto was nothing like dull ... just simply by being very scary. This was one occasion when being on a vulnerable little two-wheeler did feel like a dumb idea, but it had to be done. The route wasn't overly complicated, but the motorway system needed constant monitoring, always looking well ahead for lane changes and faster traffic cutting in on you. When you have a city of five million people, you'll always have a fair few of them out aggressively rushing along the arterial routes that we needed to follow to make our way through from the south to the north of the city. It seemed simple that we would just keep our speed steady in the inside lane, but we then found the inside lane would sometimes become the 'second out' lane as another joined inside it and yet another. I swear that at one brief point we were five out on a 10-lane highway with cars and trucks all over us, most wanting to go faster than we were comfortable with. I could feel the pressure as my eyes were trying to take it all in, watching the mirror, looking for Myles, watching my speed, watching the lane positions, watching for signs. It was a matter of just gritting my teeth, hoping and trusting that, today, the other drivers were not keen to be delayed by running over these two little 40-year-old motorbikes and their easily squashed riders. I love motorcycling and the challenges that it throws up sometimes, but this was one of those occasions when I just longed for it to be over.

Toronto behind us, the day dried up a little and the countryside began to be seen a lot more. It wasn't undulating enough to be interesting as a ride, but the farm buildings and the like kept us all mildly curious. The barns were the appealing traditional American-style that we don't have at home. The road followed the coast of Lake Huron but didn't always allow views of it. I don't know if they were, but I would describe a lot of what we passed as mangrove swamp. During the afternoon, we paused at a truck-stop diner, and to our disappointment this wasn't any better than day before. Myles and I lingered over our repast, then perused the notice board advertising for drivers while Kitty wandered off to explore. We found her down the road a bit outside a two-storey 'haunted house'. Together, we all hesitantly made our way into this abandoned home. It was brick, substantial and quite ornate, not very old. Inside, it showed signs of having been squatted in, but mostly now it had been stripped. The surrounding grounds were unkempt with waist-high grass, and it seemed as though this was an instance of the occupants having just walked away. There were no 'for sale' signs, yet basically it was a good condition house. It did now need a lot of work, replacing the floors, repairing the stairs etc., but it was OK. It was a bit forlorn, with no neighbours but the truck-stop half a kilometre away. Perhaps it had been a small farmlet, as there were out buildings away a bit. Myles the builder would have bought it in a flash if it was at home and somewhere more salubrious. Later, we fuelled up at the presumably

aptly named Coldwater before calling it a day at the South Bay Kings Portage Park camp. This was just a few kilometres off the highway on a tributary of the lake and was a small place with just a handful of campers in motor-homes and cabins. We were met by the woman owner and a dog that she said wasn't very well, as it had been bitten by a rattlesnake that morning. New Zealanders and snakes do not go together as we and Ireland are the only two countries that don't have them, or so we are told when we are growing up. Consequently, most of us are very afraid of snakes. We were reassured that they were more scared of us than we were of them … actually, I don't know how they measure that and don't think they are right.

We found an idyllic spot to pitch our tents in a small clearing with a privy nearby and picnic tables aplenty. The area, as with most of what we

had passed to date, was verdant and moist-looking. Within minutes, Myles had the Thermette boiling water for a brew. This wasn't the first time, as he had signalled dawn each day with it at Mid-Ohio, but seeing the curls of smoke stirred the feelings of 'intrepid man' in me. It always felt like we'd thrown away the trappings of civilisation and were wilderness-bound when the Thermette was brought out. It became a comforting trip staple … hearing the twigs crackling and the flames flapping and flicking, then the water bubbling and hissing when it overflows. Myles is a master with this device – no failed fires, no huffing and puffing on bended knees, no accelerants. It is almost like a signature tune.

A small road ran up past our small clearing, which led away to another more isolated spot. A little family group came walking by and told us of just having seen a rattler slither across their path. They pointed where it had gone, and it was the grassy bank behind our privy. This made going to the toilet a little more daunting. We were told that they are called pit's pigs – presumably this is because they are an American pit viper. This was our first night out on the road on our own, and it all seemed pretty good. After eating, we wandered along the stream/lake edge as the sun fell away and the half-moon rose quite spectacularly. Before it got dark, Myles had found a wooden love-chair-swing, which he was very taken by, and we photographed it for possible replication later. We strolled until it got dark, then crawled into our nylon cocoons for the night. Kitty and I shared one, and Myles had the solitude of having another.

I recall the night as being cold but not brutally so. Our start next morning was a bit sluggish.

This day just showed us that Canada is big and fairly empty. We can only judge that part of Ontario that we travelled through, and it didn't seem affluent. We passed other deserted houses and even complete motel complexes. The riding had not a lot to entertain us with, so when a billboard or hoarding would proclaim an upcoming feature like somewhere to stay etc., that was something you clung to and counted down the kilometres. In the early afternoon, when we had just about ridden as far as we felt comfortable with in the session, almost at the gritting teeth stage, there appeared a large dominant billboard telling us that 30 km further on was some eatery, the name of which has now slipped away. At regular intervals, more tempters were there at the roadside to sustain us and our numbing bums. It seemed a long 30 km before finally into view hove the promised eatery ... hove, hove! Imagine our devastation when we found this was another example of the failing economy of the region. It was big, and maybe once glorious, but now it was an abandoned shell. Our disappointment was tangible, but spirits were soon revived when not much further on we happened upon Jeremy's. This was like an oasis, with numerous cars and trucks haphazardly parked outside – almost like the urge to get inside had overcome the patience required to park properly.

Jeremy's, sadly became the benchmark for the nadir of poor dining. It was awful. We tried to like it but everything was appalling. I can understand a place like this, in the almost-wilderness, not having much on the menu to appeal to the vegetarian. After all this is where all the lumberjacks lumber. These macho men in checked shirts would at least be demanding good food that people like Myles would like ... wouldn't they? Perhaps Jeremy wasn't listening, because appalling as my meal was, Myles's was no more appealing. Of all the meals partaken during our trans-American ride, this is the one that I can remember with the most clarity. The menu had nothing that looked even the slightest bit vegetarian except for ... on the kids' menu ... macaroni cheese. This is not something I have on a regular basis, but it could be quite nice I thought. I think the young waitress did think this a little strange, a grown-up ordering macaroni cheese, but the deed was done. What was delivered brought on paroxysms of laughter. A meal with, what had to be the cheese, a bright orange rubbery stuff covering what was identified as little pasta 'elbows'. This bore no resemblance to macaroni cheese as we know it. The bright orange rubbery stuff was ... very bright orange (even more orange than the old McLaren racing cars) and very rubbery, probably like a McLaren racing car's tyres. Maybe those fabulous race cars were the inspiration. There was no pretence ... it tasted like it looked. The little pasta 'elbows' didn't redeem the meal either. The whole thing was hideous and only rescued by the fact that, coming from the children's menu, it was mercifully a small portion. Jeremy's had promised so much and delivered so little. Jeremy's took on the mantle of being on top of the dung heap of crap meals we endured. That infamous position was challenged on many occasions, with several pretenders to the throne going close, but Jeremy's was never bested ... not that we knew it would pan out that way at the time.

We found a camp in the early evening not far out of Espanola, a mill town where we'd sourced supplies for the evening meal. It had been a bit of a one-dimensional hick town of about 5,000 people, but we'd found food and found the slightly sleazy liquor store. (Subsequent research has thrown up the fact that the woman who played Miss Moneypenny in the James Bond films had lived there for 18 years – one might ask why!) The camp was administered by a middle-aged almost elderly woman who Myles christened 'the cadaver'. She was I suppose a bit gaunt and also a bit androgynous. She was also pretty upfront with her request for money, as I remember, and telling us a few camp rules. She charged us $28, which was a bit on the high side in our humble opinions. We could, of course, have voted with our wheels but chose to stay. The camp was flat and featureless, very manicured and OK in a 'it-would-be-much-better-if-it-was-full' sort of way. But it had trees and grass, so really we shouldn't complain. It just wasn't very homely or welcoming. Myles gave Kitty another haircut, which is a poor description really as there wasn't much to cut. She put the No 2 comb in the clippers and he buzzed off the No 3 length stubble. Later she trimmed up the side bits herself with a No 1 comb and then forgot it was still in place as she ran over the top one last time. Pretty drastic, but also on her, just pretty … and nice to run your hand over – like a soft furry animal. We met and chatted with a cyclist who had set out from Alaska and wouldn't be seeing his family for another couple of weeks. It was his 55th day on the road, and he was a little down in the dumps as a knee was giving him gyp. I talked cycling with him, even though I felt my puny 1,300 km two-week ride around part of New Zealand's South Island, hardly qualified me to wash his chamois.

Another slow morning start followed before we slipped into 'another day at the office'. Ride until uncomfortable, rest awhile, have morning smoko, ride again until lunch … just like work. We were quickly becoming comfortable with the new routine, that of being travellers. By lunchtime we'd reached Sault Ste Marie (pronounced Soo Saint Marie … I think), which is yet another large bridge entry to the US. We weren't to dally, but Sault Ste Marie is interesting in that there are two cities with the same name. One is in Ontario, Canada, and the other in Michigan, USA. They are old, in fact the oldest city in all of the Midwest of the US. Founded as one city in 1668, they were separated into two in 1797. We found the info place and enjoyed sitting around in the sun waiting for something that I can't remember now. We could see the giant International Bridge a few kilometres away, and it looked to us that there was a car fire or some-such on it. We could see that the traffic didn't seem to be moving, and even looking through the video camera on full zoom, it still looked like the flaring fire was on the bridge. This puzzled us, as we could then make out the vehicles slowly getting to go past the conflagration. Later we found that it was just an optical alignment of a gas flare behind the bridge. Had us convinced though! There are locks here that enable the shipping to bypass the Sault Rapids. This allows water travel from Lake Superior to the Great Lakes below and is the world's busiest canal in tonnage that goes through annually. There are local bulk carriers called 'lakers' that can be 1,000 feet (300 metres) long, and whilst they can pass through the Soo locks here at SSM, they can't get through the Niagara bypass locks between lakes Erie and Ontario so they are land locked and can't get out to the St Laurence Seaway and the Atlantic beyond. Those boats that can are smaller and are called 'salties'.

The International Bridge is a steel-truss arch bridge nearly 3 miles long which prompted Myles to praise the continent with the utterance, "One thing the North Americans do well is bridges!" We got to observe the

bridge quite close up for quite a while, as the queue of vehicles grinding their way across tailed back right over the bridge so the transit was slow. I suppose this was only to be expected, seeing this is a border entry point. Sometimes, we could skip a few places by going up the outside between the cars and trucks when there was a gap in the oncoming traffic, ducking back into the line when something came along. It was still slow though. The slowness gave me the opportunity to watch an amusing incident unfold way below in a carpark area near the water's edge. An enormous leather-clad female bikie couldn't get onto the back of a Harley. The rider sat there patiently while she tried all sorts of methods. Whether it was her obesity, or the restricting clothes I don't know, but she just couldn't do it. She couldn't swing her leg over the little backrest behind the seat, and she couldn't seem to come at the bike from the side with her leg raised up like a dancing Cossack. Finally, the rider had to get off and lean the bike over onto its propstand. He then got her to put one foot on the near-side pillion footrest, and with him pushing her bottom, he shoved her ignominiously up and into place. He then had to come hopping in like the afore-mentioned dancing Cossack because he could no longer swing his leg over in the normal fashion because she was now in place. And that got me another 50 m or so across the bridge with a smile, lessening the frustration for a couple of minutes.

Finally, we were in Upper Peninsula Michigan. The main part of Michigan sticks up like a thumb, with Lake Michigan on one side and Lake Huron on the other side, whereas Upper Peninsula Michigan sticks out of the top of Wisconsin and leans over the top of the main part of Michigan. There is a five mile gap between these two parts of the state, but as before, they crossed the water (Straits of Mackinac) with a bridge. This isn't where we were going, as that would have just completed a circle back towards Detroit etc. No, we were going to carry on past the turn-off and continue along the coast of Upper Peninsula Michigan and into Wisconsin for a short while, before turning right and arrowing straight east-west to the Missouri River and St Paul. The *Zen* ride was only a couple of days away.

Upper Peninsula made the small part of Canada we had ridden through look rich and wealthy in comparison. This part of the state looked very down at heel and poor. The scruffy rural residences all seemed to have a surplus of battered pick-up trucks in evidence. The road was tree lined with with unkempt scrub half hiding sheds and trailer-homes. My mind turned to the Michigan Militia. This is the sort of place where these die-hard paramilitary survivalists would live … far away from the federal government agents. The countryside somehow seemed unfriendly, which may have been unfair because we really didn't linger to see if it was otherwise. We filled up at a remote gas station and dallied a while at the bar, which was where you paid for the fuel. It seemed a little unusual and slightly bizarre that the bar sold gas or, put the other way, the gas station sold beer. They didn't seem to be big on drink-driving issues out here in the wilds. The tavern, as it was labelled, was a rustic board-and-batten single-storey men's refuge. The inside was dimly lit, the walls were covered in hunting photos and posters urging, "Instead of hunting for your kids, take your kids hunting." There were also 20 or more trophies lining one wall, including a large bear standing tall on two legs with a couple of cubs at her side. I found it fairly distasteful, and Kitty, who believes strongly in animal rights, said nothing. Apart from the bears and deer of all description, there were also stuffed turkeys, which seemed odd as I didn't think they were wildlife to be hunted and displayed, I thought you just bought them at the supermarket. Of course, there were the usual muscle car posters with smoking tyres and Budweiser adverts. There were few patrons, just three 'old boys' sitting at a table and one person seated on one of the impressive new-looking bar stools that were lined up at the serving counter. They seemed to be leather with a contoured bottom and a small backrest. Comfy looking, they were adjustable and plushly sank a little on a hydraulic post when you sat on them. Myles said they were tellers' stools (he'd project-managed the refit of a chain of banks' facilities), while Kitty declared them as 'pretty executive'. A sole bear cub was positioned on the wall opposite that of its family, and it looked lonely. For us, it wasn't a warm and appealing place, and we weren't tempted to linger longer than the time it took to down a solitary beer.

The roads were straight and featureless, the countryside seemingly empty of animals but filled with trees, the lake only occasionally glimpsed. The one benefit of roads like these is that the miles slip by quite quickly, and the distance that can be travelled in a day is quite substantial. Tiring in the late afternoon and happy that we'd crossed a border and still done a good mileage, we started looking for somewhere to stop and rest. The small fishing town of Manistique (pop. 1,300) didn't really appeal with its big signs for casinos and glitzy motels, but the day was nearly done. With hope in our hearts, we pulled over at a large complex that didn't have the seemingly obligatory three-storey-high neon sign and enormous flags. Sadly, this proved to be another sign of the poor economy of this area … it was abandoned. About five miles past Manistique, we came across the Aloray Motel. Subsequently, looking up their modest website, I find three spellings of their motel – Aloray, Alo-Ray and Al-O-Ray. This was an older, smaller-sized motel complex, lined along the roadside with humble looking units. There were a couple of cars already there, and the fact that it didn't have an enormous neon sign out front decided it for us … we'd stop the night indoors. The price was right and the place small but cosy. The cars turned out to be 'plants', put there by the owners to make it look like at least someone stops and stays. Possibly it worked, as one other person stayed the night. I think we bought a cake or something from their pretty humble bakery. The sign outside the motel encouragingly said "Bake Goods Pasties". These people were not scholars.

Next morning, we chatted with the owner who shared quite a bit of

his plight with us. We'd commented on the deserted places we had seen and noticed also his place had a small 'for sale' sign outside. That had been there for four years without attracting any nibbles. 10 years earlier he had left a $70,000 a year job to buy the motel. Now things were grim, his turnover was down to $28,000 a year, which hardly met their costs, and nobody was yet interested in buying. They were stuck, unable to leave but not really able to stay, the only redeeming grace being that there were always plenty of places free for when the grandkids came to visit. The price of petrol seemed to have stopped the outdoorsy folk from driving upstate to go fishing and hunting any more. We'd already seen evidence of the poor state of the economy in the Detroit area of Michigan. It had seemed astonishing to see a plot of maybe five acres, filled with 200 or more motor-homes, which is what we'd seen earlier in the ride. You just knew that some of those would never be sold.

We paused in Escanaba, a middle-sized town (pop. 13,500) that was gearing up for their annual street parade later in the day. Early-morning folk were putting out deckchairs to reserve viewing spots. Locals we spoke with talked of this as a real highlight in their year. We couldn't stay, which is a shame. It never seems fair that a community is judged as we fleetingly speed by. We don't go to their museum, find out why they are there or see the sights. I feel a little guilty about this, but it is the nature of this particular adventure. Maybe next time I'll just wander unrestrained by time or future work commitments. As we passed through, I noted a large abandoned factory near the town centre. Maybe once upon a time this was the reason for the town, but now the signage was faded away to nothing, unable to be read. It had occupied a city block each way when in use and now just lay empty and abandoned. Time and time again, we were to encounter reminders of how mighty America's manufacturing sector had been ... and how much of it had now been eroded away.

Earlier, when driving in Ypsilanti with Pat, it came over the car radio that Ford was to close 200 plants in Michigan. This was sobering for me, as I wouldn't have thought that they would have 200 plants, but apparently there are hundreds of little plants making various components. Detroit really was 'mo-town' in times gone by, a colossus of automobile production, but now seemed as though it was something from a long ago past. As an outsider who hadn't ever had the products of General Motors or Ford as part of my life, I could only wonder at the success that they had previously enjoyed. Looking at it subjectively, I could see now that having an industry based in the often bleak, wintery north must also have some downsides. Mankind is, after all, mankind. Surely they hunker down and go into survival mode every winter. I can't picture them whistling a happy tune and pushing out Chevy after Chevy at the same rate as in the summer, even if the plant is heated. Life isn't. The other thing is that many of their products are simply ... dull and old-fashioned ... stolid. It is a long time since we've been exposed to all of the US motor industry's products in New Zealand, so my observations were new and fresh. The US makes impressive pick-up trucks, they make the odd good sports car, but they don't make commuter or shopping-basket cars and their family cars are generally hideous. Modern cars are mostly appealing to my eyes, whether they are from Italy, France, Sweden, Germany, Korea, Australia, Taiwan or Japan. But looking at American Police cars for instance, and looking at the cars of the law enforcement agencies elsewhere shows who has the slab-sided dull-looking cars that no one could envy. In Europe, they have Jaguars, Porsches, Volvos, Saabs and BMWs … cars that the public covet. It was interesting to me that I'd seen that same dull shape before, with its blunt front, slightly drooping, matched engine compartment at the front and trunk at the back and the flat sides. The big Russian police cars are very similar looking. Not the small Ladas, but their full-sized cars are the same ugly style. Who was copying who I wonder? One of the Taiwanese car manufacturers had also gone down this style-line for a short while. Once learning that no-one bought them, while they had a choice, the manufacturer soon fell into line with similar sleek shiny models rivalling the other Asian models. Maybe if the US car giants started to make snazzy-looking, efficient cars to rival the others, there would be demand not dwindling sales. Then also, around the world, their cars wouldn't be dismissively labelled 'Yank tanks'.

Time was limited, and we were now closing in on the real reason for being on the road. If all went well, today we would reach the twin cities of St Paul and Minneapolis. There is very little romance about sitting on a motorcycle and riding along a straight, featureless road. There is none of the 'dancing on wheels' that a windy road brings, there are no skills to exercise, no exhilaration that accelerating and braking can bring on a sports bike. There are no views that suddenly open before you and close behind when you have passed. The vista hardly changes from hour to hour. There is no one to talk with or music to listen to. You are your own company, and solitude becomes your only companion. Sure, I had Kitty up on the back and she could give me a squeeze from time to time, but really, the time is there to be spent thinking and dreaming and scheming. We'd turned inland, crossed into Wisconsin and ridden more or less due west for hour after hour of slightly undulating countryside. We mainly followed Highway 64 through Merill and Medford, the three of us lost in our own worlds. Pirsig had his alter-ego Phaedrus to help him challenge all those philosophers in his cerebral world, but whilst I think and dream all the time, my thoughts are shallow and not disturbing to me. I still enjoy these times, however, despite the boredom.

Late afternoon, we finally reached the St Croix River (a tributary of the Mississippi River) just a little north of St Paul at Stillwater, which is over the border and in Minnesota, our third state on two wheels. This was quite a surprise to come upon, as it was the first US town that we'd come across that was visually appealing. This was where we were to turn south-west for the 20 mile ride to St Paul itself. This town of 15,000 people is known as a centre for antiquarian bookstores, antique shops and cafés. We did fleetingly enjoy the colonial architecture and people dining at sidewalk eateries as we passed through.

Our lack of detailed planning and foresight showed up a bit this day as we allowed the afternoon to descend slowly into confusion and chaos. We'd ridden well into St Paul, and having seen no accommodation places on the way in, we finally started asking for camping sites. By now, we were well inside the city limits, and no one seemed to know where to direct us to. Finally a youngish man (incorrectly as it turns out) tells us that the only camping was out at a state park. We didn't mind that but were disappointed to find we had to ride many miles back out of town. We went back what seemed in our fatigued state to be half a day's ride and made our way down a long tar-sealed twisty drive into the nice looking Afton State Park. There were lots of picnic tables and trees and a group of young Jewish kids playing and having fun while their parents socialised in the gentle way of their ilk. What did confuse us a little was a sign that pointed away from the car park area to the tenting area. This was noted as being five miles away and not accessible by vehicle. There was no way we could leave our bikes and tramp off five miles carrying our tents and cooking equipment etc. We figured we would wait until the church group departed and then we'd put the tents up and camp on the nice grassed area just by the car park. We duly did this and were happily cooking up an evening meal when the park ranger arrived. Sadly for us, he felt that rules were rules and our colonial charm wasn't going to sway his decision to kick us out … not even for one night

He did say there was a regional park that would probably allow camping and it was about 15 miles away. He was a little unsure about it though, because he was a 'state' park ranger. He said that with an inflection that seemed to infer a superiority, which we probably should have acknowledged. We decided it would be best if Myles dropped the tents and continued cooking the meal while Kitty and I would investigate the other park. There was no other option. The 15 miles seemed longer, as it always does when you are hoping to quickly find something. It is the 'watched pot' syndrome. The ranger station at the other park was closed, but we found ourselves a spot that we'd be able to put the tents up at. It was fully dark when we finally returned to Myles, and so by the time we made camp in the St Croix Bluffs Regional Park, it was very late. The day had been long and frustrating at the end but had a last quirky episode to give us all a chuckle. Myles is a true aficionado of beer, and for some reason this night, we didn't have his favourite Heineken but O'Brien's or O'Grady's or some-such Irish-branded beer. He'd enjoyed a few of these while we were away finding the other camp and then topped up when we were settled at the new camp. Just when he had arrived at a nicely mellow and merry state, he found that the beer was a 'no alcohol' one. It was nice to go to bed with a laugh as the final act of the day.

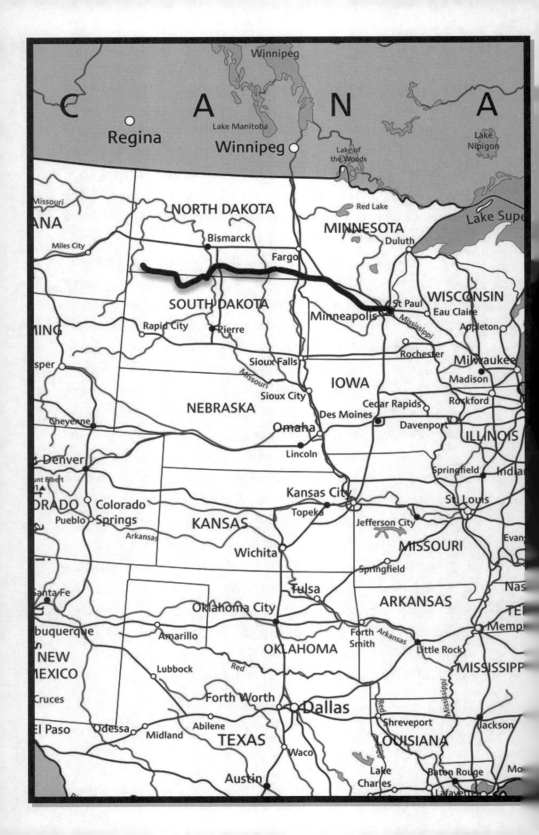

Chapter Four

ZEN AND AWAY

Although this was to be our first day on the Zen ride, there were still a few things to do before the special moment at Pirsig's house in St Paul. Myles's Honda hadn't really been fully sorted before we left Ypsilanti, and when time allowed, the remaining minor things were adjusted. Today, there was a little fiddling done in the leafy surroundings of the park before we rode back to St Paul. A flat battery meant the Honda needed push-starting, but that was OK, and using the magic of the GPS, we made our way to the nice suburban street where the Pirsigs had lived in the late 1960s.

It was a nice two-storey house with a portico entrance, shuttered windows and a large front lawn. It was late morning, so already we were quite a bit behind our predecessors who'd set off not much after sparrows' fart. Following a bit of filming, Myles suggested we knock on the door to see if there was anyone home. So

with Kitty a pace behind, eye to the lens of the Sony, I hesitantly did so ... and to our amazement, the door opened. A laughing John Curry greeted us with, "I know what you are here for ... you're not the first!" It was purely luck that John was home on this morning. He was gracious and generous with his time. He invited us in and showed us the basement workshop where there was a cupboard unit with drawers on wheeled runners – something that Pirsig had made during his time here. He also showed us the sitting room where the Pirsigs entertained during the 'hippie' era ... sitting around on bean bags, supposedly. John told us that his librarian wife was very interested in ZAMM and the history of the house so had been in touch with Ted Pirsig, the younger brother of Chris. It seemed Ted had a troubled youth here, often jumping out of the upper-storey windows to go out drinking. He is now an avant-garde artist in Hawaii. Ted is hardly mentioned in ZAMM, and I wondered if that had anything to do with his subsequent behaviour. Probably, it was just the result of the disintegration of Pirsig's marriage and the family unit. John helped us with taking photos, enabling the three of us to be in the same photo. Enjoyable as this interaction was, we really needed to get under way.

We'd been following minor roads with low traffic volumes since the dash through Toronto so the St Paul/Minneapolis experience (3,500,000 people) was something of a shock. Somehow we managed to get lost on the highway system, missing a turn-off, looping around and missing again, getting very confused and not getting onto the highway we wanted for some time. We had to do 50 miles or so on Interstate 94, which hadn't been there 40 years earlier, but now couldn't be avoided. There were no secondary roads (that we could find) going where we needed to go. This tested us a bit and it was a relief to leave the high volumes of faster-moving vehicles near St Cloud, have a belated lunch and ride another hour and a bit on a smaller road to Staples, a town of about 3,000. This is where we would get on Highway 210 and start crossing the plains to get into North Dakota later in the day. We'd then truly be in the wheel-tracks of the Pirsigs and Sutherlands. It might have been on this road that Sylvia Sutherland had seen the sad commuters that she spoke about on that first day:

The first one looked so sad. And then the next one looked exactly the same way, and then the next one and the next one, they were all the same ... they looked so lost. Like they were all dead. Like a funeral procession.

This wasn't their first-ever motorcycle adventure, as the Sutherlands and the Pirsigs had ridden together often. It is, however, a nice formalisation of the sense of liberation tinged with sadness that we all feel when we see others trapped by life's routine. You're free but they're not. I often wonder if they are aware of their plight. In my youth, I had done a cadetship, which initially was based in a 16-storey building with a large paved courtyard at the lowest level. Each evening, from high above, I would watch the ant-like figures disgorge from the sole exit out onto this courtyard ... where they would fan out and scurry off in different ways to another life. But I knew that, in 18 hours time, that same opening that they fled from would be sucking them back in again. Their freedom was only a temporary state. It was like they'd been let out on long invisible wires, and come morning, some fat controller somewhere would flick a switch and they would all be reeled back in again. I sensed that this life would not be for me forever ... just as I knew that, for many, it would be. At the end of four years I cut that wire.

We refuelled in Staples, and when in the process of paying, I had the alarming realisation that I had left in Pirsig's house my copy of ZAMM and also my folder containing the detailed maps and info about the ride. This was a calamity, and again I felt terrible and embarrassed about it. So far, I had demonstrated a resounding level of personal incompetence, and the trip was still in its infancy. After struggling unsuccessfully to get help from the store staff and very confused about what to do next, I returned to the bikes to see Myles having an apparently enjoyable chat with a young man. This was not particularly unusual, as the bikes, and in particular the Honda, always attracted some attention when we stopped. "Is that a Dream?" they'd often open with. "My brother had one when he was young, sold it when he went to Vietnam." Telling them it was a Super Hawk would bring nods of partially recalled knowledge. This time, Ben, the young man, had wandered over for a look and in the course of conversation Myles mentioned our plight and Ben replied, "Maybe I can help!" This was more than serendipity – this was the sort of thing you dream of happening when things go wrong. You couldn't script it into a movie because everyone would exclaim, "That wouldn't happen in real life!" Ben was a worker from the courier company FedEx in St Paul who'd been out for a drive, and his next work shift was starting in the early evening that day. He indicated that he had just enough time to go to John Curry (fingers crossed that someone was home), pick up the goods, go to work, package them and dispatch the parcel to Oakes, where it would be for us tomorrow. He was amazingly cool about this. He was just a really friendly guy who had clicked with Myles in the few minutes they had chatted while I was inside forlornly trying to find a telephone number to ring John. Ben just wanted to help. How good is that? He also offered us the use of his mobile phone when we couldn't get a coverage signal on the one Myles had bought in Ypsilanti at RadioShack. This introduced another bit of confusion because his phone was the same make and model yet got a clear signal whereas Myles's one didn't. We'd only been able to get coverage near big towns or tourist places like Niagara and had been living with and adjusting to this handicap as you would a minor sports injury. You're pissed off but can't do anything about it … a bit like the weather. "You must have a faulty phone," he told us. "These are quite good."

With Ben the saviour, heading back to St Paul, we surged out onto the real ZAMM roads. We merrily clipped along Highway 210, angling a little southward at Henning, straightening up again at Vining and keeping going due west past Clitherall Lake, Battle Lake and Wall Lake before reaching Fergus Falls where Ben had told us we might find a RadioShack. It was hot but OK, the road interesting enough. On their first day, Pirsig had been thrilled to see red-winged blackbirds flying from the marsh grass and, in the way of motorcyclists the world over since the beginning of this way of travelling began, whacked his pillion's knee and pointed. Chris shouts back, "What?" Pirsig shouts back an unheard "Blackbirds!" This ritual of shouting and not being heard is something we live with, although many modern motorcyclists clamour for personal intercoms. Others reject them fiercely. Often the not-understood shoutings last until the object evoking the attention of the shoutee has long since gone or been left behind. On this occasion, young Chris finally understands and stands up to shout back that he'd seen lots of the blackbirds, apparently not particularly impressed. We saw what weren't the same blackbirds but probably the great, great, great, great, great grandkids of them. This was the first occasion to be able to think of the book and go TICK … one down. We also saw off in the distance herds of bison or buffalo, we don't know the difference or if there is one. Quite a thrill, as this is another animal specific to North America that had only been seen by us previously in a zoo. Another tick went into the memory banks even if it wasn't in ZAMM – maybe it should have been.

I like something Pirsig says on the very first page of ZAMM as it agrees with the contentment I often feel when on two wheels. I sense that Pirsig was an intense man, yet he penned:

I'm happy to be riding back into this country. It is a kind of nowhere, famous for nothing at all and has an appeal because of just that. Tensions disappear along old roads like this.

Our stop at Fergus Falls threatened to bring back tensions, as it was hot now we were stationary and there were delays at RadioShack. Many phone calls were made and some of the time we left Myles to do battle there. Kitty and I waited in the carpark and engaged in conversations with interested passers-by. One in particular wanted to express his negative feelings about his government, and almost everything they had done in recent years. He was pleasant but his views a bit extreme, the sort of person who is nice to talk with, whose views you almost agree with, yet you feel unwilling to scratch the surface and engage further because of what you are sure will find. I went in and out of the mall several times, finding Myles struggling a little to keep his cool. He was being told that there was nothing wrong with the phone. It seemed that the same phone, with the same provider, had vastly different performances … depending on the way you paid for the calls. If you had a pre-paid set-up, your coverage was very poor. If you had a contract your coverage was good. We didn't have a permanent address in the US so couldn't have a contract agreement. It seemed ludicrous to be penalised for paying your way before you spend. We argued and made no progress. We were miffed that we hadn't been told our phone would be practically useless because of the back-roads route we were taking. We'd enjoyed being able to text home when in Ypsilanti, not knowing that, moving away, the phone would be as useful as having two tin cans with a string stretched between.

Our stay for the night was to be Oakes in North Dakota, which was still a hundred miles away, so the delays in Fergus Falls annoyed us a little. It was now touch and go whether we'd make it by nightfall. We pressed on resolutely, passing through Breckenridge and soon into North Dakota. Not only did the road change from 210 to 13, which confused us as we kept going due west, even though the road was 'odd', but the countryside changed as well. Not for the last time, we noticed that the state line seemed to be aligned with a geographical change. Fleetingly, we crossed over the tail of the Red River Valley, which lies north/south from inside Canada and was a 'British' area until 1818. The land was starting to look a bit more cowboyish, which added to the exotic feel of the day. We'd left behind the trees of Michigan and Wisconsin and the swamps and lakes of Minnesota, moving out onto the plains, As the twilight began to dim, after a long barren stretch of riding, we passed through the tiny hamlet of Gwinner, which for some reason made me think of Featherston back home, just a little rural town. We were just 15 miles from our destination, but it was now getting dark and Myles's Honda no longer had a headlight that was working. He was OK with following me until we reached a long stretch of roadworks that lasted for several miles, and the dust made it difficult to follow closely but dangerous to fall back. This wasn't a great end to the day. Finally, we left the main road, passing a military airfield and reaching the main street of Oakes which crossed our path at 90 degrees. It was left to the motel (by the GPS) and right to the lit area of town. We had a look at the lit area first to check there was a place where we could eat or find food. A large old-fashioned diner with slender columns supporting the pressed-tin, ornate ceiling, was still lit up. Harry's was more or less closed, but Harry himself was there and willing to feed us. We found the motel and dumped our gear before returning for something simple to

eat. We were pretty spent and pleased that the day was over.

A rest day followed, where we did just that, but also walked around the leafy town, went to the library and sent off emails while we awaited the arrival of the FedEx package. Myles did running repairs on both the Honda, which was still running a little rich, and also his 50-year-old Trapper Nelson pack. He had a sewing awl with him, and demonstrated he was a deft hand at a lock stitch. I look at Pirsig's lists of things he took and note that he didn't include an awl. He had a lot of other things but not an awl. I think that Pirsig would be what today we would call anal. When I first heard this phrase it was in the extended version of anal retentive, which would have literally meant 'full of shit', but the use seems to now mean 'overly focused'. He appears to be what the English would call 'an anorak' after the clothing that birdwatchers and trainspotters wear. He is a list maker (which in my next life I am going to be). He splits up the needs into clothing, personal stuff, cooking and motorcycle stuff and keeps a file of this. When it's time to go camping, he just gets out the file and ticks it off. Shame he missed the awl though, and a pity that his pants didn't split or something. I notice that he lists army trousers because of their durable nature and because they don't show the dirt. I ride in them also for the same reasons but in addition because they have two zipped pockets and four domed pockets as well as the usual two back pockets. This largely does away with the need to carry a small rucksack. You do need a strong belt or braces to keep them up though.

We ate again at Harry's and Kitty and I admired a tiny electric truck that was parked outside with a few tools aboard, It had a futuristic pod as a cab and plastic doors. Kitty proclaimed it as something that Bob the Builder of kids' TV fame would have. In comparison to the huge pick-up trucks that abound in this area, it was a tiny and novel alternative. It wouldn't surprise me to learn that it was a figure of local ridicule as Americans do seem to love convention, and convention appears to dictate that most items of desire should be very large and rugged-looking, not cute and quirky. Pick-up trucks here always look like they could carry the carcasses of an entire family of grizzly bears which the Marlboro-smoking driver would presumably have dispatched barehanded.

At the end of the day I chatted with two builders who were also staying at the E & I Motel. I asked them for their favourite tool and favourite tip for my *Builder's Mate* publication back in New Zealand. I'd done the same in Samarkand, Uzbekistan, and liked the thought of again showing folk from more exotic places than our people are used to seeing. I also asked what people did around the area and got the response that quite a few people went back to Gwinner for work. Gwinner had been the little town (800 people) we'd passed through just on dark the night before. Surprisingly, this is the home of the Bobcat factory. For 50 years, these stubby little rubber-tyred digger/loaders have been made here in North Dakota and exported to every corner of the world. My crystal ball gazing sees them as being a victim of their success, and I cannot see them still being in Gwinner in 10 years time. Because they are so good, they have spawned copies, and now why would we buy the real thing in New Zealand, for instance, when there are cheaper copies emerging from Japan, Korea, Taiwan and, I am sure soon, China? The logistics of building these little workhorses in Gwinner must be terrible as all the raw materials and componentry has to be freighted to North Dakota for assembly, and when they are completed, they have to be trucked off to the major freight centres. This tiny town of 800 people, way out in the wops, has a factory that employs 1,000 people (yes, people do travel to get to work). I just see that, one day, it will all get too hard, and a Ford-type announcement will see the end of Gwinner as it is today. Sad.

Pirsig wanted his journey with Chris to be like a Chautauqua, which was a travelling tent show that pre-dated the radio. These popular talks were intended to:

… edify and entertain, improve the mind and bring culture and enlightenment to the ears and thoughts of the hearer.'

Pirsig recognises that you don't have conversations on motorbikes, and while I might call it my Fantasy Land time, he writes:

… you spend your time being aware of things and meditating on them. On sights and sounds, on the mood of the weather and the machine and the countryside you're in, thinking about things at great leisure and length, without being hurried and without feeling you're losing time.

He wants to share the coming time because:

We're in such a hurry most of the time we never get much chance to talk. The result is a kind of endless day-to-day shallowness, a monotony that leaves a person wondering years later where all the time went and sorry it's all gone. Now we do have some time, and know it, I would like to use the time to talk in some depth about things that seem important.

For me, I've just always jokingly called my rides with friends and family a 'travelling roadshow' and this is just a nice chance to be able to share one and its resulting memories with a friend and a loved daughter.

In 1968, they were on the road early from Oakes for the half-hour ride to Ellendale to breakfast, and so were we. We had my package and there was reason to stay longer. It wasn't the cold ride that they experienced, but it wasn't very warm. Ellendale was quiet and only slowly waking, which was a little surprising as it was Wednesday, and by 7.30 am, many places would be bustling with people going off to work. John and Sylvia had appeared angry and cold on this morning when they reached the restaurant for breakfast, refusing later to leave until they warmed up. Pirsig wondered how they get through the Minnesota winters. John decide to put on all the warm clothes he had and cheered the group up when he appeared in his long-johns underwear shouting "CHICKENMAN!" In a sign of the more gentle times, Sylvia told him to get his clothes on or they'd all be in trouble. John strutted about some more exclaiming:

"Oh no, oh no, they wouldn't do that. Chickenman and the police have an understanding. They know who is on the side of law and order and justice

and decency and fair play for everyone."

Our GPS readings for the Nodak Café didn't quite seem right, but there it was and we enjoyed a pancake breakfast, more or less noting where the Sutherlands would have waited, warming up while Pirsig strolled around the small town, greeting the early risers and admiring a farmer's new pick-up truck, looking in a Quonset hut and finally sitting and admiring his motorbike. When it was time to move on, we found that the diner had recently moved to this location, and the old Nodak Café was just around the corner. We pose for photos outside the real deal with its flowery, almost hippie-era sign that is still there, before heading out into the parched countryside. Soon we were riding at a steady mile-a-minute pace, initially across a nearly flat landscape that was the pale washed-out tawny colour of a puma, broken only by the metallic chrome blue of numerous little lakes. The road was a long grey strip stretching ahead over the now gentle rolling land for us to follow. Unusually, it had black tar repairs, making zebra-like random stripes across it and sometimes along it, never more than 3 or 4 yards apart. We presumed these repairs were as a result of frost-heave splitting the road surface. Mile after mile, we shuddered across the small ridges made by these black stripes. It wasn't the rhythmic clickety-click of a train journey but it was quite similar, with a side-effect of being quite hypnotic and very hard on the eyes. I pondered briefly about the link of visual repetitious impacts and epilepsy.

The day quickly became very hot, and the landmass began to roll gently up and down. This was the High Plains. It was an interesting day because, despite having travelled across many countries, including some of the steppe of Russia, this was unlike anything I had crossed before. The shimmering grasses, the tiny lakes and glare-induced mirages all contributed to making a landscape of surreal beauty belonging on an old-fashioned biscuit tin. By the time we reached Hague in the late morning, the temperature must have been close to 100 degrees Fahrenheit. For the

last 20 miles before Hague, we passed groups of cyclists, some reaching Hague before us. There was nothing open in Hague, which is really just a dot on the map, with less than a hundred residents. It may have been bigger in 1968, because it was here that a pair of goggles was bought for Chris, as the hot dry air was burning his eyes. The cyclists were on a four day ride around North Dakota, and this was a turn-around point where they'd head north and we'd head south. Straight ahead of us, 25 miles away, was the mighty Missouri River. The riders arrived in dribs and drabs, eagerly grabbing the drinks made available by the organisers. There seemed to be several hundred cyclists and why the locals didn't take advantage of their passing was a mystery to us. Opening up your shop to sell beer or any cold drinks would be a bonanza, but Hague was like a ghost town that day. We mixed and mingled, interested in their adventure and endeavours, with many of them interested in ours. There were several family groups, and

this added to the pleasant nature of the stop. A number had recumbent lay-down-style bikes, which I admire and one day hope to have. Our bikes both had New Zealand stickers on them, and this always triggered a comment, today being no exception.

Pirsig must have been travelling without a map, because in Hague, he asked the petrol attendant if there is a way to cross the Missouri nearby. There was now no petrol dispensing in Hague, so we moved on, to try and get some cooling air moving around us. We were now riding south, parallel to the Missouri, but still 30 miles or so east of it, out of sight. We passed through Herreid where they'd paused briefly for a drink. Somewhere near here we passed a sign that had the distances in kilometres as well as miles. This was unusual in that we had seen no other like it nor did we again. Mentioning it later to others, always brings a look of, "Are you sure?"

Now we were in South Dakota, and after a long and rough detour, we stopped at Mound City with a population listed as 89. The gas station

owner told us "that was a while ago" and that now it was more like 65. The gas station was an old light-blue corrugated-iron clad barn-like building from where they repaired all things mechanical and also sold spare parts and thankfully cold drinks and ice blocks. There was no canopy over the pumps, no shelter. It was now as hot as it gets … baking hot. We lingered inside in the shade after paying the affable woman who turned out to be the co-owner with her husband. They'd come here in 64 as young marrieds, she told us, buying the place in 1968. They'd have been there when Pirsig's Chautauqua went through. "Are you going to the casino?" she asked. We shook our heads in the negative. It turned out that going to the Indian casino up past Mowbridge, was the only entertainment for many miles. In her work clothes, this matronly woman looked nothing like a casino-goer, not that we'd been to one in this country. She told us of her success, pointing to a large-size cheque on the wall. It was made out for $5,000. She also showed us other ones she had kept in a file. Presumably, she'd had the

money but been allowed to keep the cheques. We asked her if she was ahead or whether the casino was the overall winner so far. Laughingly she asserted that she led easily, but her husband called out to the contrary. They both agreed that it was their leisure activity and wouldn't give it up for anything, there being so little to do in this relatively remote backwater.

We also sheltered in the shade of the little brick Post Office opposite. We'd gone across to admire the murals at the insistence of our new friend. Mickey and Minnie Mouse were featured on the window next to the door, a Harley motorcycle on the next window and around the corner, a large bald eagle and a depiction of Lewis and Clark, the famous explorers. They'd been sent off by President Thomas Jefferson to try and open up a water transport route from the East Coast to the West Coast. When Jefferson dispatched them in 1804, he expected they'd encounter woolly mammoths, erupting volcanoes and a mountain of pure salt. His letter of appointment notes, "The object of your mission is to explore the Missouri river, and such principal stream of it as by its course and communication with the waters of the Pacific Ocean whether the Columbia, Oregon, Colorado or any other river may offer the most direct and practicable water communication across this continent for the purposes of commerce." This expedition was known as the Corps of Discovery and was to take more than two years. They were only the second group of non-indigenous people to cross the US from one side to the other. We were to encounter their journey several times as we crossed Montana, often following the Missouri. Ironically, I have been told by an authority that they never went to Mound City despite being depicted on the Post Office (presumably for the 200th anniversary). Of course, there wasn't a Mound City to go to, and the location is only 20 miles across the land from the river and maybe they roamed that far when hunting. They did definitely go to the area now known as Mobridge.

The 50 mile ride down Highway 83 to Mobridge was more of the same. It always seems harder when there is a goal ahead like, in this instance, lunch. Finally, we rolled down the slope of the main street of Mobridge, noting a motorcycle shop and a bright yellow painted diner. Mobridge looked alive and bustling. It was a bigger town than we've seen for a while, having a population of about 3,000. It is a crossing point of the Missouri so is always busy with through-traffic. It is also an important cross-roads. We could have kept riding south on 83 to Pierre, the capital of South Dakota, but that was not our mission. Myles wanted a special screw to be able to refix his visor to his helmet, so we decided on bike shop first, diner second. At the bike shop, I noted a couple of travellers needing a bit of attention and talking to the service guy. The young middle-aged male rider had a Suzuki V-Strom a sensible all-rounder as a bike, which means it isn't seen often in the US where most bikes on the road are Harleys or Harley-clone cruisers. The other rider was a short woman and she had a Suzuki Bergman scooter of 400 cc. She was asking about a new drive-belt, I think. They were from Canada and had been on the road for three months.

The bright yellow diner turned out to be memorable for only one thing, and it wasn't the food. We found a recruitment flyer for the National Guard. To our outside eyes, this document was very dated in its nationalistic fervour, urging the youth to join up to "save America from its enemies".. The pamphlet's zeal was tangible, and I was a little shocked to read about being specifically trained to kill those enemies. I think it goes without saying that, by joining the military ... any military ... you will be trained to kill someone, somewhere, somehow – but we found it a bit distasteful to see it put so enthusiastically. We could also see that, for many kids growing up in these tiny little settlements in rural America, if they weren't able to afford to go to college or perhaps didn't have the smarts, this would be a way out. There would be a certain appeal at age 18 in being paid to leave the fairly dire employment predicament most rural kids would find themselves in. None of what we'd seen so far of America had been the slightest bit like what is portrayed on television or by Hollywood. It was generally gritty and lacking the affluence and contented happiness that the celluloid world exudes.

After the initial excitement of crossing such an impressive river on an impressive bridge, the euphoria faded quickly. The 150 mile ride that afternoon just reinforced our thoughts about how big and empty America can be and how hard it was to be relentlessly riding across it on 40-year-old motorcycles. It continued to be scorchingly hot, and even though there were nice cloud formations in the sky, they never seemed to come in front of the sun to give respite. The clouds did give Kitty something to photograph though. Tonight was to be a camping night, something that young Chris was so keen on earlier in the day and which Pirsig resisted initially, citing the lack of tree cover and lack of water in this sort of country. State Highway 12 took us back on a northerly arc away from the Missouri but back up to and then along the state line with North Dakota. Our

camp spot was to be Shadehill Reservoir about 18 miles out of Lemmon, South Dakota.

Lemmon was notable for two things, one being the quaint, petrified-forest local museum, which was nice and folksy ... in a funny, country way. The other thing was our brush with Mark Resner. Mark had been driving along when he spotted the two bikes going the opposite way. He looked at them first as a fellow motorcyclist, then realised what they were because of his passion for ZAMM. He just knew that putting a 1965 BMW and a 1965 Honda together in Lemmon just had to be a *Zen* ride, and that is what he excitedly greeted me with as he came running towards me. "It's a *Zen* ride, it's a *Zen* ride isn't it!", a grin a mile wide on his face. "Tell me it's a *Zen* ride!" Mark is a ZAMM enthusiast who has done several portions of the ride without yet finding the opportunity to put it all together and complete a pilgrimage. He has three copies of the book. One for under the seat of his bike, one is kept in the car, and a special limited edition good one that his wife got for him remains safely at home. He also writes for a local newspaper, so did a little interview with us. He explained where we should camp and further explained the reasons why he felt other Pirsig pilgrims usually camped elsewhere on the Shadehill Reservoir road. He had local knowledge and told us how it would have been back in 1968, and we were happy to run with his suggestion as it cut a few miles off the ride. Just like the others, we were tired, but this time we were probably a little ahead of them. They had only an hour of daylight left when they stopped in Lemmon.

It was near dark when they made camp and struggled with cooking and later eating. A wind had sprung up, and it made cooking their steaks difficult, as the flame wasn't getting close enough to the meat. Later, sitting in the shadow of the light thrown by their headlights, they couldn't see what they were cutting or eating. Chris spilled his meal on their tarp, then wouldn't eat it, saying it was dirty and he didn't like the taste of it. They were all tired, there was no other food, and Chris walked off having said he wasn't hungry and his stomach hurt. Sylvia was concerned, but Pirsig told her that the sore stomach had often happened before and he'd been examined many times, including for appendicitis. That spring, it had been diagnosed as the beginning symptoms of mental illness. Pirsig admitted to having stopped the psychiatrist sessions because they were not kin. He knew he couldn't hold out for long but still felt that only kindness and understanding could come from kin (this was probably a reaction to his own mental health treatments). He told them of a sad poem by Goethe that ends in the death of a child, a ghost the winner. It was a not a merry night and Pirsig commented"

Here life is the end and ghosts have no meaning. I believe that. I believe all this too." He looks out at the darkened prairie. "although I am not sure what it all means yet … I am not sure of much of anything these days. Maybe that is why I talk so much.

Our night had none of these dramas. We made camp, cooked up, explored a little and had a peaceful evening. The Canadian travellers Dianna and Barry from the bike shop back in Mobridge turned up on their bikes so tales were told and experiences swapped. They were not a couple, but just good friends who had decided to have a road trip together. They'd wandered gently and well. I was a bit envious of their flexibility, knowing that our time-constrained ride, would always be compromised by my need to reappear at work on a given and immovable date. After we'd eaten, Kitty went over to their camp and had a long enjoyable chat with them. She struck up a rapport with Dianna in the way that so often happens on the road, making an arrangement to later stay with her in Canada at the end of our ride. Kitty was heading for a yoga ashram that is not too far from Dianna's place, and a brief and interesting sojourn would result. She would even get to work for one of Dianna's female friends as her builder's labourer. But all that was in the future. Not only was the campsite pleasantly sited, but there was a water pump, trees, picnic tables and fireplace … and within a short walk there was a diner with internet access. This was a sophisticated part of the wilderness experience.

Our camping already had a routine to it because of the days at Mid-Ohio and the pre-*Zen* ride to St Paul. The mornings began early and I usually just sensed Kitty slithering away out of the tent while it is still dark outside. When I come to think of it, it was just as dark inside the tent, especially as my lids were always closed at the time. Kitty liked to have a period of meditation each morning, but didn't like holding us up. Myles also rose in the half-dark. His pattern of enjoying a few beers at night (helped him sleep he said) always resulted in his middle-aged bladder forcing him from the sleeping bag for relief at an early hour. These were both things that happende while I was blissfully away with the fairies, rescuing damsels in distress, before winning the Isle of Man TT races or playing for our beloved All Blacks (New Zealand's national rugby team). I half-woke to the crackle of burning leaves getting the mighty Thermette going, and at 6.00 am, the flap of the tent was gently drawn aside, and a cup of coffee pushed in. This was room service at its finest. I always felt a little guilty though … a bit of a lie-about, stay-in-bed person, even though it was still only just after dawn and not always warm yet. Myles's non-battery-driven awakening system could be something that speleologists (cavers) adopt, as I gather they have to take alarm clocks with them when overnighting in caves. Normally, our bodies sense dawn and wake accordingly. When it remains pitch black, our eyes/brains must periodically have a quick surreptitious peep and go, "Mmm, still dark, still sleep time." Apparently, without alarm clocks they can remain curled up in their sleeping bags for more than 24 hours. They need the discipline and reliability of Myles's bladder.

We were going to leave ZAMM today and experience the craziness that is Sturgis. I've enjoyed the experience of paralleling Pirsig's tale so far, reading it each night to try and get a feel for the next day's ride. This is the easy part of the book, entertaining and informative. It is gently thought provoking. This night at Shadehill Reservoir after Chris had his outburst, Pirsig had a disturbed night where he slept only fitfully, and while I was happily enjoying near super-human exploits in my somnolent world, he saw a figure in a fog that he recognised:

> I am about to say something, to call to it, to recognize it, but then do not, knowing that to recognize it by any gesture or action is to give it a reality that it must not have. But it is a figure I recognize even though I do not let on. It is Phaedrus.
>
> Evil spirit. Insane. From a world without life or death.
>
> The figure fades and I hold panic down … tight … not rushing it … just letting it sink in … not believing it, not disbelieving it …but the hair crawls slowly on the back of my skull … he is calling Chris, is that it? … Yes? …

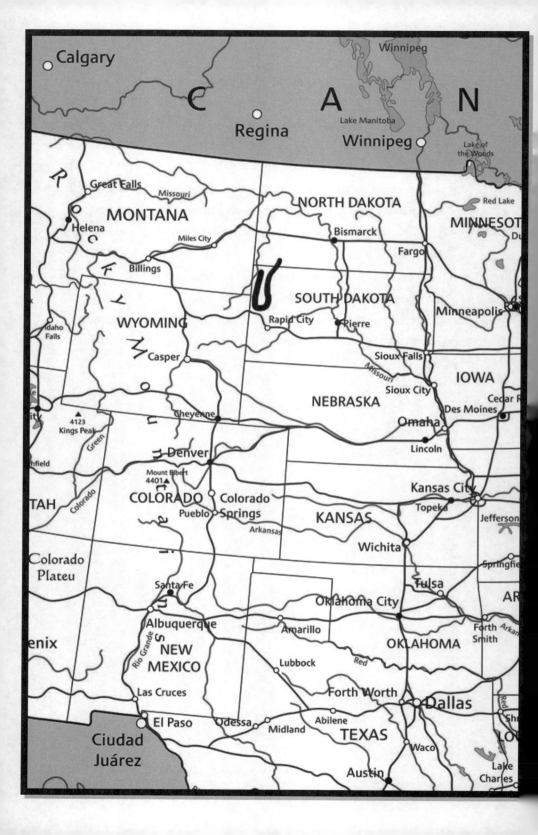

Chapter Five

TEMPORARY CITIZENS IN STURGIS

This was a good time to leave the book for a bit of respite … the calm before the storm. It was getting a bit heavy … the philosophy was starting to intrude more and more. Phaedrus is Pirsig from earlier mentallytroubled times. It is Phaedrus who gives this book its depth and who for many provides the exhilaration that makes ZAMM a way of life as much as simply print on a recycled tree. Phaedrus gave me so much trouble in my earlier readings. I hoped that with this being the third time round, I could enjoy rather than suffer his deep philosophical ramblings.

Dianna and Barry decided that the orchestrated display of hedonism that Sturgis promised to be was not for them and they headed on slowly back towards Vancouver … with no set itinerary, no set pathway. We were partly envious, but pleased also at being able to do what we are doing. It was a quirky experience not having a real choice in where we were, what we did and where we stopped. Being on Pirsig's pathway was an easy option. But today it was for us, we were in control. This was like Friday night,when you are first approaching adulthood. We were excited, we

didn't quite know what to expect, we were hopeful of exquisite enjoyment yet still unknowing of our roles in this pageant. Would we be participants or merely spectators … voyeurs? Is there such a role? Our plan was to leave ZAMM and ride due south back into South Dakota on highway 73 the 170 mile to Sturgis. We'd stay a couple of days possibly, and then ride north again on a parallel-running road 50 miles further west, regaining ZAMM at Bowman. This would give us all a break, as I knew ZAMM would only get harder from here on, now that Phaedrus had arrived.

The ride south was interrupted only by a photo stop to capture a tiny boundary rider's hut, which I later captioned 'little house on the prairie' and a short break at Faith (pop. 489) where we met and chatted to a tall, statuesque female rider from Alaska, just beginning her ride home. It had taken her six days ride to get to Sturgis, she'd had her fun, and now it was time to start for home. Myles needed a few minutes to play with the , so a bit of shade was found opposite a run-down church with the message outside "Ch_rch, the only thing missing is u" which tickled us a little, seeing as where it was. Surprisingly, this was sheep country. We didn't see many but whenever we stopped, the New Zealand stickers brought

forth comments about Kiwi workers who'd spent time in the area shearing. As we'd become accustomed, it was hot and we probably looked an odd pairing with me riding with a long-sleeved jacket on to keep my freckled-skin from frying, whilst Myles aired himself in the breeze, often wearing just a blood-red tee-shirt on his torso. We did always wear helmets unlike the majority of American riders we passed in this part of the US. Now we were encountering lots of bikes and soon learned the simple bikers' greeting of the road. Being that we were riding on the right-hand side of the road, it meant that our 'spare' hand, the middle-of-the-road hand, was the clutch hand, which was not already engaged keeping the throttle open ... leaving it free to wave or otherwise acknowledge the riders passing the other way. At home in New Zealand, our spare hand is not the one nearest to the passing motorcycle so greetings always seem remote and often we just resort to a nod. Here in the US, it was *de rigueur* to simply use your free hand to loosely point to the road, leaving your arm in this position until all of any group of riders pass. The others would be doing a similar action and your outstretched, down-pointing arms at times passed perilously close. We mightn't look stereotypically cool, lacking the splayed leg stance and ape-hanger arm positions of the boulevard-cruisers we seemed to be passing, but we've got the discreet greeting off pat. Possibly Sturgis would teach us more in the ways of the cool.

The event we just knew as Sturgis had been running for a few days already this year, so as many people were riding away from Sturgis as riding towards it. Subsequent statistics showed this, the 66th Sturgis rally, to be slightly smaller than the recent ones with the attendance dipping under the half million for the first time in a few years. Six years earlier, the numbers peaked at 660,000 (the population of the state of South Dakota is approximately 750,000). This year there were five deaths and 89 marriages. Oddly, the number of births isn't recorded, but 589 tons of rubbish were collected, only 324 parking tickets issued, the sheriff's office received 1,217 calls and there were 447 hospital emergency room visits. The oddest statistic kept seems to be that there were four tickets issued for illegal handlebar heights. I wonder what they are, and I wonder if anyone other than the ticket issuer knows it. I don't know how hard they were trying, but there was one fewer felony/drug arrest than illegal handlebar height tickets … only three.

For a town of 6,000 to host 600,000 bikers means some amazing things have to happen. You can't just ask the locals to 'put up' a guest or even billet a gang of 20. Enormous campsites spring up, purely to host the hordes for this one week. It has evolved into something very professional. It is now an event of some magnitude. To entertain the attendees, headline bands of international repute are engaged to perform. We missed Tom Petty, Joe Cocker and Stevie Nicks by one night, but every night had acts of similar calibre … but none of it was cheap.

Quite a few roads converged as we neared Sturgis, which is in the Black Hills of South Dakota, the Badlands, not all that far from Mt Rushmore and the famous sculptures. Despite us being so close, on a probably, once-in-a-lifetime ride across the US, we didn't take up the opportunity to view these landmarks. It all seemed too hard and too hot at the time. The roads were collecting and intensifying the numbers of bikes, until we were riding with others as we reached the turn-off to our camp just before the township. It was noticeable that not many were carrying luggage. They were probably day-trippers. Our camp was less than 10 miles from town, one of the closer camps. It was not big in terms of Sturgis size but at 40 acres, in our eyes it was massive. I had been expecting this to be a sea of canvas (I know tents are now nylon, but the words don't run), but instead we were greeted by more motor-homes than we could imagine existing. Camps like this hold tens of thousands of people and almost all of them come in motor-homes. The riders who actually ride to the event are such a small minority as to almost be insignificant and mostly invisible. This could be a reason for the absolute lack of shade in our camp.

The young woman at the gate welcomed us and told us there were regular courtesy shuttle buses to take you to town so you can drink as you'd wish. She did temper this advice with the news that a person the night before had bumped another and been 'stepped' outside when the bus stopped at the next stop and stabbed to death. There was also gossip that there'd been a shoot-out at another camp between the Hell's Angels and some other gang, resulting in at least one death. Some welcome! We found a flat spot beside an enormous 'fifth-wheeler' trailer, and after putting the tents up, we sheltered in its shade. Our camp had plenty of toilet and shower facilities, a shop and a bar, but no trees for as far as we could see. It was only early afternoon, so we went for our Sturgis experience. We decided to enter into the spirit of the day by going helmetless. We didn't have the cloth 'durag' bandanna to tie around our heads and look really cool, but hey, we were here as spectators, not as players. As soon as we left the gates of the camp we were in an informal parade of Milwaukee's finest. We were probably the only non-Harleys for miles and miles. Myles was amused and bemused to observe that, on his little Honda, nobody would ride next to him. He felt he was like a motorised pariah. It is hard to record on paper that booming, syncopated sound of hundreds and hundreds of vee-twin motorcycles. A few years earlier, Harley Davidson had tried unsuccessfully to patent their sound, which is often portrayed as a 'potato, potato, potato' sound. As many of the show-ponies strutting their stuff had no exhaust muffling at all, it was a thunderous roar that rolled into town. Every intersection saw bikes lined up to criss-cross the two main routes that the bikes would roll up and down 24 hours a day. After an enjoyable couple of miles through and back, we parked up. We'd ridden alongside all sorts of poseurs. Kitty filmed and we chatted as we rode. She even managed to capture a pretty young thing in her skimpy gear putting on her lipstick as she rode pillion along the main road through

town. Huge numbers of young women were riding in bikinis, the bikes mostly customised works of art.

The town was heaving with humanity. The bikes lined up were memorable for their diversity, colour and imaginative workmanship. Very few standard bikes were on display, which is why so few were ridden any distance. This really was a 'show and show' rather than 'show and go' event. "If you've got it, flaunt it," seems to be the mantra. It was nothing to do with motorcycling really. It was about showing what you had either created or had the money to buy. You had to be bold and often brave – no shrinking violets were to be seen here. There were stunning displays of man, woman and machine. It was an eye-opener to see a beautiful, curvy young woman in a skimpy polka-dotted bikini wearing stiletto-heeled boots riding a matching polka-dotted heavily chopped Harley. To be slightly crude, the lady had balls. We bought freshly squeezed lemonade from a tanned young thing squeezed into what she'd normally be at the river in. We also went to a fairly sleazy bar … we were people watching. Some of it was quite funny because you knew that a good 95% of the people here, wearing their 'bad to the bone' gear, getting new tattoos, drinking to participate etc., were acting out fantasies and back home were probably legal clerks or dentists.

It was fun but it was shallow. There was only so much play-acting and street theatre we could take, before we want to express ourselves. I longed to shout a wonderful expression of the English ... "Tossers!"

We'd noticed the large numbers of men and women wearing bandages and I thought a hell of a lot of people must get into fights but was then told, it was the covering of a new tattoo. Kitty poked her camera in an open window from an access lane and interviewed a guy getting a tattoo ... not his first, it was a huge eagle and 'live to ride' like a Harley advert. The tattooist had a sign there proclaiming, "Show us your tits, free beer!" This was not a classy festival by any means. Kitty doesn't like beer, so no show for the ink man. We also couldn't resist going into The Knuckles Bar, a two-storey, bare-fist arena catering for impromptu 'no-holds-barred' fighting. It was gladiatorial with the crowd lined around above the ring,

baying for blood. We arrived at the time of a 'chick fight'. This had men throwing money into the ring until several hundred dollars were up for grabs and young women from the crowds were enticed into fighting for it. Surprisingly, Kitty wriggled her way to the front downstairs and filmed a fight from close-up. Myles and I felt that, by being there, we were almost participating or approving and only watched for a short while before moving on to another bar for another rest out of the sun. Kitty also interviewed one of the gun-toting motorcycle Policemen on his Harley. He felt things weren't going too badly

so far. We perused the sales stalls with Kitty buying a couple of 'durags' to send home as gifts. We resisted the tasselled leather crop-tops and gee-string thongs. There were some amusing tee-shirts for sale, others highly inappropriate, some crude and funny, but some just so crude you were embarrassed to see them on display. Sprinkled among all of this were the real one-percenters ... the few with a hardness of stare, the challenging looks and swagger ... the ones you could tell really were the living enactment of many of the trite slogans on display.

It had been a sight to behold but as we still had our bikes in town, we couldn't drink to excess, so rode back to camp where of course there was a bar and later a reasonable band. We enjoyed a bit of time with Marlow, Heidi and Vance, the family in the trailer we sheltered beside again. They're regular attendees and come from up near the Canadian border. They ride some of the way and take turns in the driving of the big pick-up that pulls the 'fifth-wheeler'. Marlow is the patriarch, a husky-voiced, gnarled old railway worker and was able to tell us a bit about the trains we'd admired. He told us that they won't put a freight train on the track if they can't fill 100+ wagons for it to pull ... and like to have up to 150. It was an easy friendship that sadly wouldn't be able to be built on, as we'd decided to move on tomorrow. We'd seen as much as we wanted to, none of us needed or desired a tattoo, we probably prefered our own company to drink with and the bikes on display were not our thing. I was quite happy to be leaving, wanting to put Sturgis behind me, because this could so easily have been a nightmare of having to sit each day in the near 100-degree heat trying to sell books and DVDs to an audience who clearly wouldn't have cared. Originally, I'd signed up for a whole week at the camp as a vendor. The decision back in Mid-Ohio was clearly the right one. I was wrong about one thing in my original planning. The half million attendees of the Sturgis rally are not, in the main, motorcyclists ... they are not my market. I could see there would be nothing about an epic ride across half the world on old classic bikes that would appeal here. An ordinary night drinking beer and watching an OK band ended the Sturgis experience. Showing our age, by midnight, we quit the festivities, unable to be enticed into staying longer by the upcoming wet tee-shirt competition.

Just a day off, and already we were eager to get back to ZAMM. Sturgis had been Sturgis – astonishing, interesting, OK, but ultimately not really us. Maybe we were not the Fun-Bobbys that we once were. Youthfully, I'd done my best at the Munich Oktoberfest, and the Pamplona bull-running San Fermin Festival, but now the exhilaration of debauchery was jaded. 30 years ago, I'd have stayed the distance, probably arriving a couple of days early and not leaving for a week after, but life does that to you, just like the tee-shirts … "Been there, done that!"

We were on the edge of the Black Hills (so-called because the pine forests from a distance looked black), so the countryside was interesting, and as we headed away north again, we got to encounter for the first time those staples of cowboy books – buttes, mesas and gulches. Disappointingly, we'd learnt that butte is pronounced beaut and not butt. Somehow, that spoiled the fun of Butte View, Big Butte, Naked Butte, Bald Butte, Dimpled Saggy Butte, Myles's Butte, Kitty's Scrawny Butte and all the other buttes. I learned later that a mesa is just a 'big' butte – one that is suitably huge, but not as big as a plateau. There certainly were some wonderful ones sticking up out of the landmass here, as we moved back onto the plains and away from the Badland hills. This is Custer and Crazy Horse country, and we paused at a couple of sites of military encounters, musing that history is only ever written by the winners. We note that when the US army or cavalry won, it was a 'battle', and if the Indians won, it was a 'massacre'.

We followed Highway 79 across a familiarly deserted landscape for a while before doglegging across to 85 to get a straight run at Bowman. I noticed at one stage that Myles was missing (sounds like the title of a kids' book), and we paused at the top of a hill to watch and wait for him. While doing so, a cowboy came out of his land on an off-road motorbike, stopping to chat. He was a sheep farmer so not really a cowboy, even though he had a pistol in a holster – just like the real thing. "That is for coyotes," he told us. His family had been on the land for several generations and I wondered to myself if he's ever seen the sea. It was a pleasant interlude and Kitty enjoyed filming the ordinary man once more. The British Law Lords many years ago defined the 'ordinary man' as being "the man on the Clapham Omnibus". The US 'ordinary man' would have me confused. Is he the fat waddler of Mid-Ohio, Ben the FedEx guy, the Sturgis duragged, tattooed poseur or this friendly cowboy on his modern steed? Interestingly, none of them fitted the TV portrayal foisted on us half a world away.

With Myles gathered up again, we pressed on until the oppressive heat sent us indoors at Buffalo (pop. 380). Just another funny little town … down on its luck by the looks, remembered by coming across a couple of road bikes – a Buell and a Honda, riding with a Harley cruiser. They were outside the bar as we arrived. Road bikes are a rarity in the US, but we didn't get to interact before they blasted off back into the country. We put the bikes in the shade against the side wall of a small, red, paint-faded log-cabin-style bar and went inside. It was dim but interesting. The walls had generations of assorted junk – harmless cowboy and drinking memorabilia, attached in various ways. A stuffed puma nonchalantly stretched out on a branch behind the bar was the main item that helds our interest. I don't recall what we ate – probably my omnivorous persona is blocking out all the vegetarian memories. As a traveller, I am not a good note taker, believing that anything memorable, will be just that and able to be recalled because of the strong impression it has made. I realise that I am a bit like that in life and hope that next time when I come back as the improved 'Des Molloy', I will be a note taker and a list maker. I'll probably have the luck to be sent back as a dung beetle though, because of all the excrement I have spoken in this life.

TEMPORARY CITIZENS IN STURGIS

119

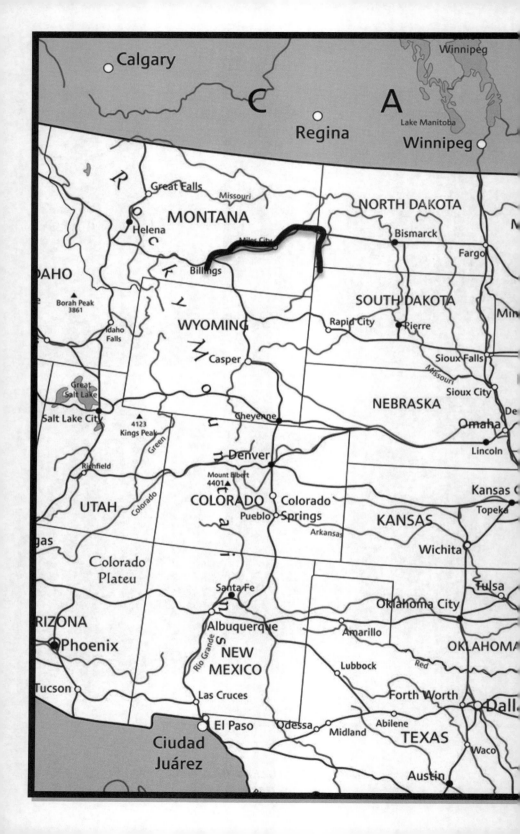

Chapter Six

REZAMMING THE JOURNEY

Early afternoon we reached Bowman (pop. 1,600) … back on track with the ZAMM crew. It impressed us as being quite a pleasant town, despite being festooned with flags. It was not just a strip of humanity clinging to a road as it passes through – Bowman had side streets, a library and even a town centre of sorts. The earlier Chautauqua, had paused here, but it was not one of their overnight stops. We reasoned however that to press on and catch up today for the right night stop would mean pushing ourselves to the limit. It would be more pleasant to have a short day, catch up with laundry and writing emails etc., and tomorrow could also be the same, as it would also only be a half day to get back in sync with our predecessors. To start with, we found somewhere for a drink just like they did.

This had been where they'd stopped. It was 102 degrees, and with beer and air-conditioning calling, an old stockman paused to talk bikes with them. He used to have a Henderson, he told them, and wanted to yarn a bit. Pirsig was happy to respond, even though he could sense the others' eagerness to move indoors. Pirsig felt that the old duffer deserved his time … if he was willing to endure the searing conditions. He admired the dignity of the old guy as he walked off, having said how pleased he was to have met them. I'd recalled this bit of the book only because of the

Henderson, a four-cylinder American bike of the 1920s. In our home town of Wellington, for many years in my youth, there had been one in a glass case in the scrap-metal dealer Curly Hansard's office. In later years, it was sold in a non-running state for the equivalent of $20,000. No Henderson owner stopped us going in for the deserved draught. What a shame! We didn't linger too long, as we needed somewhere to stay the night. There was camp due east, we were told.

Just out of town, we found the empty, be-flagged camp having followed the sign to Butte as instructed. After establishing camp in a nicely grassed area with hedges for shelter, I made an initial sortie into town, while Myles again tinkered with the Honda. The library had a most helpful and pleasant young woman who was a wonderful credit to her upbringing and environment. She was both charming and competent, at ease with both the young and old who came through during my time there. We'd done most of the libraries, as we'd moved across the US. The back roads we've been travelling on didn't have the backpacker travelling clientele that has seen the emergence of the internet café This institution has sprung up almost on every corner in cities and towns all around the world ... but not on the ZAMM route. In their absence, here the libraries gave free internet access, which of course stifled demand anyway. This wonderful service kept us in touch with our families and friends back home. Sometimes, we visited and just send off a message ... and sometimes I had a 'dispatch', which in the words of the numerous 'wide-mouthed frogs' who bring us cooking shows and the like, "I have prepared earlier". My pocket-size Palm One PDA and fold-out keyboard were still in my eyes, a perfectly adequate way of penning what I must and so much easier than trying to carry a laptop computer with us.

The librarian was interested in our journey in a personal as well as a professional way, and she told me of their local enthusiast who writes about old bikes ... and how he had helped with the library's featured display, which is motorcycling. It was a fascinating presentation with old posters advertising local race meetings and lots of old flyers, catalogues and brochures. Many I hadn't seen before and it was a nice encounter. Just as she was closing, the old-bike enthusiast walked in and she introduced me. He had one of my favourite bikes, a Velocette, but his main interest was in bikes of the very early 20th century. His speciality was a particular one called a Wagner (made in St Paul for a short while from 1904). His card proclaimed him to be a 'purveyor of motoring ephemera'. Some Americans do have a way with words. Of course, it could also be said that many don't, and the dearth of book shops in small towns may be contributing to this.

Back at camp, we gave Kitty a motorcycle lesson on the Honda. This was accompanied by not too many shrieks, and she showed an aptitude that augers well for one day having her own freedom machine. Two small families arrived with what, back home we call scamper-campers, a pop-up towed caravan of much smaller scale than we had seen before in the US. This was it for the night, many acres for us all to play in should we so feel. A crone came and took down the flags, and gave us a bollocking for not seeing and filling the honesty box. We'd presumed that a ranger of some sort would arrive just like before. We placated her with money and all was well. A weather front came across and brought rain and briefly hail. This was the first precipitation we'd had since our Niagara day. It was refreshing and cooling but didn't last long.

We went into town for our evening meal. Our files showed that the Lone Pines Steak House would have been where they slaked their thirst and had a beer. This may or may not have been true, but the only place that the ephemera man has pointed us to was Big J's, an unusually modern, sterile place with photographed meals and matrons in uniforms. Everything was a bit formulaic and pre-packaged, like aircraft meals. The woman serving us was quite good fun and my soup was OK. What lifted the night as far as being notable was finding the Zen Ride 2004 stickers left on the door by a couple of German Harley Davidson riders. We'd been aware of their ride, but here was evidence, which made it more real somehow. Framed as a noticeboard was a copy of the cover of ZAMM and the couple of pages relating their Bowman experience. Cool! Later, we snuggled down into our nylon cocoons and made it through a very blustery night, our first since being on the road. We had another leisurely day ahead of us, just half a day's ride.

While we'd been away, Phaedrus had been coming to the fore. Phaedrus is interesting and also a bit scary. He is never really explained to us, so what I take from him may be completely different from others' interpretations. He is both Pirsig's mind as well as his past. It is as Phaedrus that Pirsig is able to explain his past, telling of his terrors and failings but also his ideas and understandings. I have always found the propensity for a certain

type of wandering American to loudly pontificate on all subjects to the minutest detail to be quite wearying it has to be said. Their intense analysis of the most mundane interests me not … and annoys me sometimes. And when they proclaim that they are trying to find themselves, I quietly wish that they were lost somewhere else. However, when Phaedrus analyses a motorbike, I have to take notice and follow carefully.

Phaedrus divides human understanding into classic understanding and romantic understanding:

A classic understanding sees the world primarily as underlying form itself. A romantic understanding sees it primarily in terms of immediate appearance. If you were to show an engine or a mechanical drawing or electronic schematic to a romantic it is unlikely he would see much of interest in it. It has no appeal because the reality he sees is its surface. Dull, complex lists of names, lines and numbers. Nothing interesting. But if you were to show the same blueprint or schematic or give the same description to a classical person he might look at it and become fascinated by it because he sees within the lines and shapes and symbols is a tremendous richness of underlying form.

I follow, but don't know if I need to know.

Although motorcycle riding is romantic, motorcycle maintenance is purely classic.

Again I follow and can agree, but am surprised later to learn that:

in recent times we have seen a huge split develop between a classic culture and a romantic counter-culture – two worlds growing alienated and hateful towards each other with everyone wondering if it will always be this way, a house divided against itself.

Pirsig tells us that Phaedrus's intense analysis was first thought eccentric then undesirable and later a little mad. The hostile opinion of him drives him further insane and the estrangement climaxes with court-ordered Police arrest and permanent removal from society. And all this is just setting the scene for describing a motorcycle. When the tedium of the ride along US 12 became depressing Pirsig was happy to reflect on the rational, analytical, classical world of Phaedrus – his own past:

He was a totally classic person. And to give a fuller description of what this is I want now to turn his analytical approach back upon itself – to analyze analysis itself. I want to do this first of all by giving an extensive example of it and then dissecting what it is. The motorcycle is a perfect subject for it since the motorcycle itself was invented by classic minds. So listen:

A motorcycle may be divided for purposes of classical rational analysis by means of its component assemblies and by means of its functions.

If divided by its component assemblies, its most basic division is into a power assembly and a running assembly.

The power assembly may be divided into the engine and the power-delivery system. The engine will be taken up first.

The engine consists of a housing containing a power train, a fuel-air system, an ignition system, a feedback system and a lubrication system.

The power train consists of cylinder, pistons, connecting rods, a crankshaft and a flywheel.

The fuel-air system components, which are part of the engine, consist of a gas tank and filter, an air cleaner, a carburettor, valves and exhaust pipes.

The ignition system consists of an alternator, a rectifier, a battery, a high voltage coil and spark plugs.

The feedback system consists of a cam chain, a camshaft, tappets and a distributor.

The lubrication system consists of an oil pump and channels throughout the housing for distribution of the oil.

The power-delivery system accompanying the engine consists of a clutch, transmission and a chain.

The supporting assembly accompanying the power assembly consists of a frame, including foot pegs, seat and fenders; a steering assembly; front and rear shock absorbers; wheels; control levers and cables; lights and horn; and speed and mileage indicators.'

And that was just the description of the components of a motorbike. I could follow with the words of the infomercial-speak "But wait … there's more!" … and there is, pages of it. It has to be a very long straight road and a very disturbed person to come up with this detail of analysis, for in the words of the masses, "who gives a shit?" Phaedrus says that to know about the motorbike you have to know the functions of the components, and further:

'there are normal running functions and special operator-controlled functions of the components.'

Of course, the romantic just likes the look of it, learns the management and rides the wheels off it – making it dance with the joy of the performance that has been breathed into it by that classical creator.

US 12 was still an old neglected road and on 12 August 2006, it was still hot, but there was no despondency in our travelling roadshow. It was a Saturday but admirably, the Bowman Library was open for Myles to send a missive home via the ether. We were pleased by that … but we were pleased by most things. Every turn of the wheels was a yard or two closer to the complete realisation of our endeavour. We were moving towards Montana and the land forms are changing again. Now it really was starting to look like a cowboy movie, the plains giving way to stronger, more dramatic, redder, craggy mesas and gullies, no trees at this point. There were canyons.

We rolled into the historic town of Marmarth, the last in North Dakota. It was tiny and seemingly untouched. I smiled as I thought ahead to the possibility of writing this book. When editing *The Last Hurrah*, my editing cousin would furiously respond to every 'tiny', every 'huge', every 'memorable' with 'how tiny, how huge, why is it memorable?' My subsequent research tells me the tiny is 140 souls. Unlike our predecessors, we paused and had a quick look around. This was a railroad town once and still had a wonderful old railway station. Myles declared that he'd like to relocate it home. It was exquisite with a patina of history evident in every scratched and scraped board, every sagging corner, every lost tile. There was also an abandoned auditorium, an oddity in a place so small. In a short dead-end side street there was even an award-winning restaurant … but it was not the right time for us, we were on a mission. We did a slow loop through unpaved streets looking on mildly dilapidated homes with the detritus of life away from the big city scattered around. Some had vegetable gardens. Old cars lay casually abandoned or left mid-repair for attention some other time. I reflected that this could be a snapshot of so many places I have travelled to. With its old American cars and red-dirt streets it could be a village in Guatemala or Mexico or even Eastern Turkey. Again, I reflected that this was nothing like the America our friends thought we were riding through. Maybe they'd be disappointed to see it, but for us it is the reverse. This was delightful. Here, there was the simplicity missing in Pat's life in Michigan. There were no gadget shops, no Walmarts, none of the frenzy of consumerism apparent. We regretfully passed on, pleased to have tasted but a little sad we couldn't stay and learn more.

For the Chautauqua, the day was a furnace, 108 degrees by the time they got to Baker (pop. 1,695). They rested in a bar, Chris pointing out a thermometer in direct sunlight was registering 120. For us the day was also hot but we're becoming used to it and maybe the edge has gone. Baker looked big and bustling after the tiny hamlets we'd been passing through of late. This really was the big smoke, it had an airport, a radio station, a weekly newspaper and a high school. It had a lake right within the city limits. We refueled at a busy gas station, indulging in a little more people-watching, fascinated by the young cowboy types trying to ape what they'd seen in the movies. But we were in Montana now, so maybe they were bred this way and were travelling through the normal passage to full adulthood.

We found it gently amusing. Being as it was lunchtime, we slid around the corner into a quiet side street and went into a fairly non-descript bar. We ordered pizza and a beer. It was cool, but as is the way here, the rooms were dark. We chatted to the barmaid who was lively, had travelled a bit and probably wouldn't be staying long. She was finding Baker a bit too small, too much of a backwater. I recognise the type and recalled a very similar young woman working for me when we had a period of living in a rural small town. Cherie was a wispy slip of a girl, but she was too big for the town. She needed to fly when all around her seemed unwilling to even walk. Her purple hair seemed to outrage the foundations of the town, so she dyed it blue to show she could … and green. She had far too much life for the stifling dowagers of the burg. A wonderful worker, we could only encourage her to run with the speed that she had. It was like the words of a Sting song: "if you love somebody, set them free." I don't know where she went, but we were so proud when she did.

We played a few pokie machines with little result. We couldn't stay and drink as there was still a bit over 100 miles to ride that afternoon. With the twilights still long and warm, that would give us a leisurely ride and plenty of time to wander in Miles City. Pirsig felt that as the temperature was so hot, they shouldn't ride faster than 50 miles per hour so as to not overheat the tyres, but the Sutherlands didn't seem to take this on board and went on much faster. Not for the first time, Pirsig lets them go and rode reflecting on Phaedrus.

He was a knower of logic, the classical system-of-the-system which describes the rules and procedures of systematic thought by which analytic knowledge may be structured and interrelated. He was so swift at this his Stanford-Binet IQ which is essentially a record of skill at analytic manipulation, was recorded at 170, a figure that occurs in only one person in fifty thousand.

He was very contemplative along this strip of road, telling us more about Phaedrus and how he didn't try and use his brilliance for general illumination but sought one specific target and focused on that to the detriment of his life.

In proportion to his intelligence he was extremely isolated. There's no record of his having had close friends. He travelled alone. Always. Even in the presence of others he was completely alone. People sometimes felt this and felt rejected by it, and so did not like him, but their dislike was not important to him.

There follows a long diatribe about the 'ghost of rationality' and wanting to take revenge on it. He weaves this in with a tale of being a hunter and how, having been without food for three days, thinking deeply but still unwilling to leave the wilderness, he has a surreal experience with a timber wolf. We learn more about Phaedrus and Pirsig's fear and fascination for him. I enjoyed reading ahead to learn what we were potentially in for, and whilst sometimes the interference by Phaedrus seemed to detract, for many, this is what gives the book its punch. When I can understand it, I am usually left thoughtful ... and glad I don't have an IQ measureable in more than double figures. I make no apologies for bringing him back at length at this point, because I feel it is important to know what went before, what the make-up of Pirsig is.

> One Friday I had gone to work and got quite a lot done before the weekend and was happy about that and later that day drove to a party where, after talking to everybody too long and too loudly and drinking way too much, went into a back room to lie down for a while.
>
> When I awoke I saw I has slept the whole night, because now it was daylight, and I thought "My God, I don't even know the name of the hosts!" and wondered what kind of embarrassment this was going to lead to. The room didn't look like the room I had lain down in, but it had been dark when I came in and I must have been blind drunk anyway.
>
> I got up and saw that my clothes were changed. These were not the clothes I had worn the night before. I walked out the door and to my surprise the door-way led not to rooms of a house but into a long corridor.
>
> As I walked down the corridor I got the impression that everyone was looking at me. Three different times a stranger stopped me and asked how I felt. Thinking that they were referring to my drunken condition I replied that I didn't even have a hangover, which caused one of them to start to laugh, but then catch himself.
>
> At a room at the end of the corridor I saw a table where there was activity of some sort going on. I sat down nearby, hoping to remain unnoticed until I got all this figured out. But a woman dressed in white came up to me and asked if I knew her name. I read the little name clip on her blouse. She didn't see that I was doing this and seemed amazed and walked off in a hurry.
>
> When she came back there was a man with her, and he was looking right

at me and asked me if I knew his name. I told him what it was, and was as surprised as they were that I knew it.

"It's very early for this to be happening," He said.

"This looks like a hospital," I said.

They agreed

"How did I get here?" I asked, thinking about the drunken party. The man said nothing and the woman looked down. Very little was explained.

It took me more than a week to deduce from the evidence around me that everything before my waking up was a dream and everything afterward was reality. There was no basis for distinguishing the two other than the growing pile of new events that seemed to argue against the drunk experience. Little things appeared like the locked door, the outside of which I could never remember seeing. And a slip of paper from the probate court telling me that someone was committed as insane. Did they mean me?

It was explained to me finally that "You have a new personality now." But this statement was no explanation at all. It puzzled me more than ever since I had no awareness at all of any 'old' personality. If they had said "You are a new personality," it would have been much clearer. That would have fitted. They had made the mistake of thinking of a personality as some sort of possession like a suit of clothes, which a person wears. But apart from a personality what is there? Some bones and flesh. A collection of legal statistics, perhaps, but surely no person. The bones and flesh and legal statistics are the garments worn by the personality, not the other way round.

But who was the old personality whom they had known and presumed I was a continuation of?

This was my first inkling of the existence of Phaedrus, many years ago. In the days and weeks and years that have followed, I've learned much more. He was dead. Destroyed by order of the court, enforced by the transmission of high-voltage alternating current through the lobes of the brain.

Approximately 800 mills of amperage at durations of 0.5 to 1.5 seconds had been applied on twenty-eight consecutive occasions, in a process known technologically as 'Annihilation ECS'. A whole personality had been liquidated without trace in a technologically faultless act that has defined our relationship ever since. I have never met him. Never will.'

Wow, that explains a lot. In ZAMM, Pirsig lays bare his soul on many occasions, and for that I admire him but don't always enjoy or eagerly look forward to more of it. The layering of the book gives pleasure on several levels, some of it a quick fix, some of it more thought-provoking, and it was now getting deeper as we crossed the continent. I have to admit to liking the road-trip writing, which is easy to read and appealingly descriptive. Is it because I agree with his expressive prose … or is it because I lack the capacity to comprehend page after page of self-analysis? I am a reader, devouring books of the 'middle rung'. I abhor 'pap' but possibly don't have the cerebral performance for the step up to the scholar's 'A' list. To me, a 'cone-head' is a 'cone-head', and there is no point me pretending to be one also. They're blessed and should be revered as such. Back a step … we're all just pub philosophers. I'm probably more opinionated than most. I do 'think' more than I 'do', which may be just a polite way of saying I dream a lot. Maybe Mum was right when she used to describe me as a *"little* Walter Mitty*"* – a fictional character of James Thurber. I laugh when now as an adult I can reference authorities like the American Heritage Dictionary and find Walter Mitty noted as "an ordinary, often ineffectual person who indulges in fantastic daydreams of personal triumphs". In my childhood, I'd not enjoyed the Danny Kaye movie portrayal and thought Mum's description was mean and a little demeaning, even though she always said it with a smile on her dial. Now I would wear it as a badge of honour.

While he pondered his past, Pirsig had fallen far behind the Sutherlands and when they pulled into a roadside stop that he knew of, the Sutherlands were waiting to ride off, furious, Sylvia proclaiming, "We're just … angry!"

and John snaps, "Where's all that stamina you were telling us about?"

Our own little travelling roadshow hadn't had any of these tensions. We'd enjoyed a togetherness that had been easy-going and informative. There had been the slow bonding of personal exploration. My past hasn't included electric shock treatment or any disorders of the mind, no spectacular meltdowns. It's been mildly predictable and responsible, mostly, not a lot to hide. Myles quietly share his memories of repairing Shackleton's hut in the Antarctic, of being a film-set boat-builder in Spain, of being the maintenance carpenter as part of a weather station team on remote Auckland Island in the Southern Ocean. We'd learn of his travels with Sandy ... his life with Sandy, his geology degree, his adult carpentry apprenticeship, his motorbikes, the kids. It was like osmosis as we slowly discovered each other. Kitty was the quietest of the three of us but didn't seem to be a minor player or daunted by our age. She and Myles enjoyed an easy companionship that wasn't forced or false. To date, we seemed to have happily agreed on the path we were following. "As soon as you aren't travelling on your own, you will be making compromises," folklore says. "The more travellers, the more compromises." So far we hadn't had to face the 'two against one' democratic decisions. We were enjoying the riding, enjoying the stopping, enjoying the thought of riding some more. I knew this would be something that will remain as a special episode in the journey that is life. There would be plenty of 'remember when we rode across the US' memories to be recalled in years to come. Our little team ha been fused together, and no matter what the physical separation, there'll always be a togetherness.

And now on the road to Miles City, we saw on our right in a roadside paddock a pair of zebras ... real live zebras just standing around grazing nonchalantly with a couple of donkeys. Of course, we stopped because this wasn't something you see every day or indeed any day. These were real zebras and not a circus in sight. Kitty raced off down the slope to the fence

to interview these out-of-place African visitors. Myles and I watched her from the roadside like a couple of doting parents admiring her technique, Sony on shoulder, whispering and cajoling. The donkeys, a black one and a grey one, who might have been mules because they were pretty big, loved her and came over for a chat, whilst the zebras just ignored her completely. No amount of fresh-grass coaxing would bring them to the fence. She had to make do with the friendly muzzling of the long-eared asses. Myles noticed that the two zebras appeared to be photographic mirror images of each other, it was as though one was a black animal that the white stripes had been applied to, whilst the other was clearly a white animal that the black stripes had been applied to. It looked like the creator had only the one stencil. This kept us interested for some time, as there was a wonderful symmetry when they stood in the right place … which wasn't often. We bet that the ZAMM team never saw zebras.

After what seemed weeks, we were finally having some sweeping corners to play on. They were not challenging, but it was an enjoyable experience to be cresting a rise and to be greeted with the road running away in a gentle downhill curve before disappearing over an inviting shoulder. At times, we were overlooked by bluffs with a line of curious conifers watching us go by. We posed Myles beneath the Miles City 10 mile sign. It was a silly but nice moment. Miles City was even bigger than Baker, the biggest town since leaving St Paul. It had 8,500 people and was on the main road so to speak. This is where we left the little state highway and had to follow Interstate 94 for a day. Our first goal wasn't hard, as the Olive Hotel was a fairly plain but imposing, three-storey, historic brick hotel on Main Street dating from 1898. Its main architectural feature was a Victorian porch and lobby of impressive proportions and style. The managers were a family, with the young teenage daughter taking an unhealthy fascination with our

Kiwi accents, thinking they were "so sexy". Embarrassingly, she would ask us to talk every time she saw us. "It's so cute!" she would squeal. This was almost like when the ZAMMers were here. The young desk girl asked if they owned the 'groovy, dreamy motorcycles outside the window.' Our unit was upstairs, in a conventional double-level motel complex just across the side street. We arranged to have free-reign of the laundry in the main hotel. While we were being directed by the shy 15-year-old son Harley, we got him to show us one of the historic old rooms. It was suitably antique in nature, and Harley told us of a ghost who still roamed the corridors. Later, he took us across the road to their nuclear bunker. We'd spotted the nuclear sign and had asked about it. The family hadn't really taken on board that this was their nuclear shelter. They had just used it for storage for years. Harley got the key and we all had a look. I don't think he had been in there before.

Miles City is where the others had recharged a little, having arrived so exhausted that John Sutherland hadn't remembered his name at check-in. They'd soaked away their fatigue in claw-footed baths, marvelling at the softness of the water, and later enjoyed a stroll down the town, feeling like family. Later, we did the same. Ever the worry-wart, Pirsig redid his tappet adjustments the next morning, probably in the area below our motel unit. Three of his four tappets were fine but one was too loose, requiring adjustment. He was pleased with finding the source of the slight noise he'd noticed before. He also whittled a stick into a suitable shape and cleaned his spark plugs with it. The plugs are sooty or as he puts it:

> ... the porcelain inside this first plug is very dark. That is classically as well as romantically ugly, because it means that the cylinder is getting too much gas and not enough air. The carbon molecules in the gasoline aren't finding enough oxygen to combine with and they're just sitting there loading up the plug. Coming into town yesterday the idle was loping a little, which is a symptom of the same thing.

I could be a little picky and say that it was the cylinder head's combustion chamber not the cylinder itself that is getting too much gasoline, but let's not engage in semantics – no point in two of us doing it. Close to five pages follow in the book, where the concept of the motorbike is addressed and the functions and components further explained, this time with a series of organograms. I can't fault it and it is intriguing in an unnecessary way. Not for the first time, I wonder if Pirsig would be a fascinating character to encounter or an incredible bore. I suspect that I'd choose our team.

There weren't many people who interact with Pirsig as they travelled, but one who did make the hallowed pages of ZAMM was Bill of Bill's Cycle Shop. The shop was open but deserted with Bill not in sight when Pirsig went there in search of standard size carburettor jets. He had finally worked out that the altitude was causing the bike to run rich, and he wanted to change the jets back to the slightly smaller ones originally fitted. I don't think he ever explained why he had the larger-than-standard ones in. Possibly he had gone in search of more top-end performance, or he may have felt he knew better than the Honda factory. Miles City is at 2,500 feet, and Pirsig's sensivity meant he could notice the difference. Knowing they'd be going higher, he warranted that the switch would be worthwhile. In time, Bill returned and had the required jets and a footrest rubber for Chris's pillion peg. He didn't have the chain link adjuster link that was wanted though. (I thought one of those was on his list.) Bill's workshop was not the sort that Pirsig admired, noting that Bill was a mechanic of the 'photographic mind' school. There were wrenches lying scattered haphazardly, with parts loose and jobs half done, sales literature and accessories cluttering the place such that there was not even space under the benches. Pirsig couldn't work in conditions like that but recognised that Bill could probably put his hand on anything needed in that chaotic space. He did snipe with a quip, though, that move one tool three inches and Bill would spend days looking for it.

We felt no inclination to follow his example in changing the carburettor's settings. Any change of performance was not easily detectable, and it hardly seemed worthwhile rejetting as there would be a need to go back to the original setting, when the altitude was lost for the California coastal riding. What Pirsig didn't explain is that if you lean off the mixture to have exactly the right combustion for riding at higher altitudes, there is a risk of being too lean when you go down off the high plateau. Being too lean is more dangerous than being too rich as the lean mixture will make the engine run hot and the pistons can seize in the cylinder bore or even be holed by the extremely hot temperature in the combustion chamber. Being too rich will just make the bike run a bit sooty, but no harm will result. Pirsig didn't mention changing back later, and I wonder if the changing of jets really took place or was it just an exercise of 'quality' for the book.

There was a restaurant called Jo Jo's as part of the Olive Hotel, and we felt no desire to venture elsewhere. It may not have been Kitty's idea of an ideal balanced vegetarian meal, but baked potatoes lifted it above what we've struggled with in many places. This was a nice night of ordinariness … we're contented. The bikes were going well, we were going well. There was a rising intensity to ZAMM, but we'd handle that as it comes or I'd do as I did when on the road, riding and reading in 1977 … I'd just skip the pages that are too hard, too deep. We had a full repast complete with pudding and coffee, then wandered slowly through the rabbit-warren-like ground floor towards the front of the hotel. This took us past a table of gamblers. This was a proper gambling set-up in a designated area. I'd seen gambling in casinos but never like this, where it reflected the past with images of smoky saloons coming to mind. Just one big table in a private alcove. There was no jollity at the table, they were all poker-faced, so to speak. It looked grim and scary to us. When they needed sustenance, food was brought to the game, the players not pausing or looking away. Food was just a fuel, not something to enjoy and savour. We watched in silence. Large amounts of money were evident and one player, more than the others, seemed to be not only losing more often but he looked like the person least able to lose. He was the youngest, the most nervous looking, slightly jittery in his movements. I felt sad that he was there. Was there a tragic tale behind this? Was it desperation, like the hackneyed plots of numerous celluloid entertainments and soppy love songs? We'll never know, but this display of overt testosterone didn't leave us all warm and fuzzy inside. It left us a little disturbed and uneasy.

Next morning, we returned to Jo Jo's for our favourite breakfast of pancakes. A stack of pancakes did so much to set us up for the day, and despite Kitty's proclamations about white flour, carbohydrates etc., she was as enthusiastic as any of us, as this had now become quite a habit. It also gave us a bit of consistency. In the main, the ingredients would be just coming out of a packet. "It's the American way!" ... thanks Pat, but what this did, is that it stopped anybody making really bad pancakes. Even Jeremy back in Canada couldn't make a bad pancake if the makings came from a packet. So, often three stacks of pancakes arrived onto the three plates of the three eager bears, who waited patiently with fork and spoon already in each hand. The Olive was no exception. Blueberry pancakes and coffee – wonderful. It may not have been healthy, but the fruit and muesli would have to wait until there was more control in our lives. This day, we also enjoyed chatting with a breakfasting roadworker, who we would call in our part of the world a lollipop lady. She held up the stop/go signs and told us of the significant roadworks up ahead. We'd already encountered this before, and I remember way back in Ypsilanti being a little surprised at Pat's concern for routes with roadworks on them. Roadworks in New Zealand and elsewhere I have been don't often result in big delays. The contractors always have to work around providing alternative access for through-traffic, usually a temporary road. Not so in this part of the US. Roadworks often meant that you stopped and waited for what might be a considerable time before a guide vehicle took you through the many miles of construction being worked on. This could be very disruptive and unpleasant in the hot times we'd been through. Our lollipop lady told us that in the pecking order, a pilot is higher than a stop-go person. They all aspired to be the one who drove back and forth leading the charge.

Back 38 years, the others had decided on a steak lunch before hitting the road. It seemed to have been an enjoyable and interesting meal. The Sutherlands had liked the town, being taken by the 'real' nature of what they could buy and the open friendliness in a bar visited earlier in the day. It is at this meal that we first learned about the significance of Bozeman. The Sutherland's related how they'd heard a tale in the bar about an occasion when the State Governor was about to fire 50 radical college professors but was killed in a plane crash before he could do so. Pirsig told them it was some time ago, later admitting that, if there were 50 names on the list, his would certainly be on it. They indicated surprise, but he told them it was an era of right wing politics, and this ws the college where even the First Lady had been banned because she was too controversial. "Who?" they chorused. "Eleanor Roosevelt." Pirsig also passed the aside to the reader that he didn't know much about it ... it had been 'him'. It iss apparent that this was their intended destination, and as they rode out of town the same way they'd come in. Pirsig wrote:

> On the way out we pass a city park which I noticed last night, and which produced a memory concurrence. Just a vision of looking into some trees. He had slept on that park bench one night on his way through to Bozeman. That's why I didn't recognize that forest yesterday. He'd come through at night, on his way to the college at Bozeman.

Slowly as the book unfolds. we learn more about Pirsig's earlier years now relegated to being the life of the half-remembered Phaedrus. We already know of the 170 IQ we soon learn that Phaedrus had finished his first year of university science at 15 but had been expelled at 17. Immaturity and inattention to studies were the official causes given. Pirsig drip feeds us more bits of his tortured background, which led finally to his personality removal. He wanders aimlessly for some years then joins the army and ends up in Korea. His letters from Korea apparently show his thinking changing and later on the troopship taking him home, he studies a book by F. S. C. Northrop on oriental philosophy. He finds it hard to read, but learns the terms 'theoretic' and 'esthetic', which correspond to what he later calls classic and romantic. There is so much that gets fed only slowly to the reader as we move through the book, yet we need to know some of it now, to know about Bozeman and the university there. Phaedrus seems to have spent some time in India and studied oriental philosophy at Benares Hindu University but left after an exchange of differing ideas with the professor. He left the classroom and left India. He returned to the Mid-West, got a degree in journalism, married and had two children. They lived in Nevada and Mexico, where he did odd jobs, but later recommenced studying philosophy, challenging every philosopher he encountered. Somehow, he ends up teaching rhetoric at Montana State College, Bozeman, but then suffers rejection in his career there. Ultimately, he suffers his destruction in the hands of the men in white coats. All of this is just giving us the background to Pirsig's impending return to Bozeman and the feeling of trepidation that keeps coming through in the book.

This was our first chilly day's riding since Toronto, and although the route necessitated riding along the Interstate 94, enabling the miles to be clocked up quite quickly, it was us, the riders, who cracked. We were cold after 150 miles. The ride had been interesting as it followed the meandering Yellowstone River, and this part of Montana had lots of trees. We encountered several long, long trains. These must have been right up there with the 120 – 150 big buggers that Marlow had told us about. Trains are nice to either run with or even pass going the other way. There seems to be a romantic link in my eyes between trains and motorbikes. They're something I like seeing moving across a landscape … and I like being in

that landscape on a motorbike to see it ... and sometimes play. All of this had been nice, but I temporarily called it quits at Hysham ... to warm up and regroup. We found a store for coffee and warmth. It was OK once we're stopped, quite sunny and a nice choice of place to stop. Hysham is a rural village just off the highway and with only 330 people, it was centred about the general store. On the way in, we'd passed a house set back from the road with a big anti-meth sign painted on the roof. We asked the local sheriff, who at some stage ended up at the store, about it and whether methamphetamine was a big problem in the area. We call it 'P' at home in New Zealand and it is just as big a problem, one that has destroyed families and even communities. The sheriff was a pleasant young man with none of the posturing that personifies some of the law-enforcement officers in this country. On reflection, that trait can be found in uniformed people in all the countries I have travelled across, and it is unfair to target the US solely. As well as the sheriff, Kitty found a young Danish motorcyclist to interview.

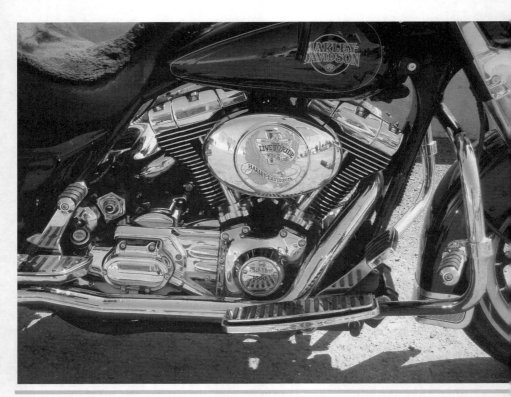

ZEN AND THE LAST HURRAH
144

He was riding around the US on a Harley-clone Yamaha. A seemingly self-sufficient, resolute man maybe in his early 30s, he gave the impression of not having come down in the last shower. He seemed to know what he was doing and quietly oozed competence and confidence. He was moving as and when he felt the need or the mood took him. Nice.

When we'd warmed up, and had a second coffee, we slowly prepared to move on. We had another 150 miles or more to go to our overnight stop of Laurel. Just as we got ready, a middle-aged couple on a touring Harley Davidson with a matching trailer hitched to it pulled in. The bike had every imaginable touring option, with chromed almost-everything and the stereotypical 'Live to ride' emblazoned on the air filter. The bike sported showy leather tassels from the bar ends, and the mirrors were aftermarket ones with flashy engraved embellishments. I found it all a bit hackneyed, but would never say so. Each to his or her own. The seats were stepped, with both the rider and the pillion having a backrest. The seats were clad in black sheepskin and looked invitingly comfortable, especially the back seat which included fold-down armrests. The trailer had camping gear lashed neatly on top. With the rider sitting behind a large windscreen, it just all looked very suited to the big distances available to the US riders, yet strangely not desirable in my eyes. We have a phrase back home that cruelly describes overly made-up women trying to retain their youth. 'Mutton dressed up as lamb' portrayed well the bike … and to a lesser extent, the riders. It was just too alien to my world and I just know I'd never get Steph on one of these glitzy behemoths, not even with the promise of a brown paper bag for wearing over her head. It was so 'not us', yet so well suited to the image-conscious American riders.

On this part of the journey a car and trailer nearly took out the Pirsigs, leaving them all shaken as Sylvia saw a cardboard box fly into the air at the same time ,thinking it was their bike. She was still churned up when they stopped for a late lunch. This part of the ride seems to have taken

Pirsig deeper into his reflections. Page after page of challenging philosophy interrupt the journey. Phaedrus explains the hierarchy of thought and the two kinds of logic, inductive and deductive. Many hypotheses are explored giving examples of six categories of logical statements relating to a cycle maintenance problem. He seems to admire and relate to Einstein, he references and explains Kant and Copernicus and he mentions Parkinson, who I presume is not the British TV presenter, and Scottish philosopher David Hume. This is hard, heady stuff, which even the most resolute must struggle with. For me, part of the difficulty is the enjoyment of the way the road trip is recorded and the mystery of Pirsig/Phaedrus's past being then augmented by an in-depth philosophical treatise. It is so wide in its scope that it seems like you're a juggler just managing to keep three balls in the air when another four or five are introduced. It is that hard. Some can handle it, but I'm really just a three-ball man.

For me, the thoughts as we droned along the highway heading towards our night's destination were much simpler, similarly reflective but much, much simpler. When the roads are dull, the scenery fixed, and no interesting machine manipulations are required, often you do sink back into a shallow torpor. The eyes are open but not much else. The cranial electro-magnetic activities sink to a minimal level. I fall back to my childhood and thoughts of my wonderful mother. Surprisingly, I ponder as to why she always cut my school lunch sandwiches straight across the middle, dividing the bread into two similar sized rectangles. My Italian schoolmates' mums cut theirs across from corner to corner making two triangles. I think it was sandwich envy that made me covet their triangles. Not only did they look better, appearing to portray style and sharp modernism, maybe reflecting the shark-finned cars their fathers drove ... but I was convinced also that they tasted better. Doing a bit of a Pirsig, I think about the 'utility' of the triangle-cut sandwiches. With three points, there is the obvious middle point to grip the mini repast delicately and the other two end points are enticingly available for the first bite. That first bite, severing the tip, is always nicer than a first bite of a middle-cut sandwich. Is it because the triangle tip severance is part crust, part non-crust, whilst a straight-cut first bite will usually be a half-round chomp into the straight face which is all non-crust? Mmmm … and another 10 miles go by. What confuses me a little is why I don't step up and tell mum that I also wanted my lunch triangle-cut. I must have been such a submissive wimp, I reflect. This brings up other maternal anomalies and perceived injustices. I'd told her once that I liked raspberry jam sandwiches, and for the next 15 years, that is all I got. Why didn't I protest for change? I think of our independent-thinking, bolshie kids and smile. I think also of the family tradition that meant there was always the first of the season's cherries on the table as a treat on my birthday. Why didn't I tell them I didn't like cherries? I muse further that now, as an adult, I quite like cherries and, by choice, I do a cut that is a compromise between the stylish Italian-cut triangles and the boring middle-cut. My cut is an almost-triangle but I do sometimes do the full triangle and sometimes the full middle-cut to reassure myself that there is a taste difference. I snigger to myself that if I ever told anyone about this, the men in white coats would soon be around asking me questions.

And this brought us to the outskirts of Billings, the largest town in Montana. We were not going to stay here, and fortunately, the roads bypass the city central area.

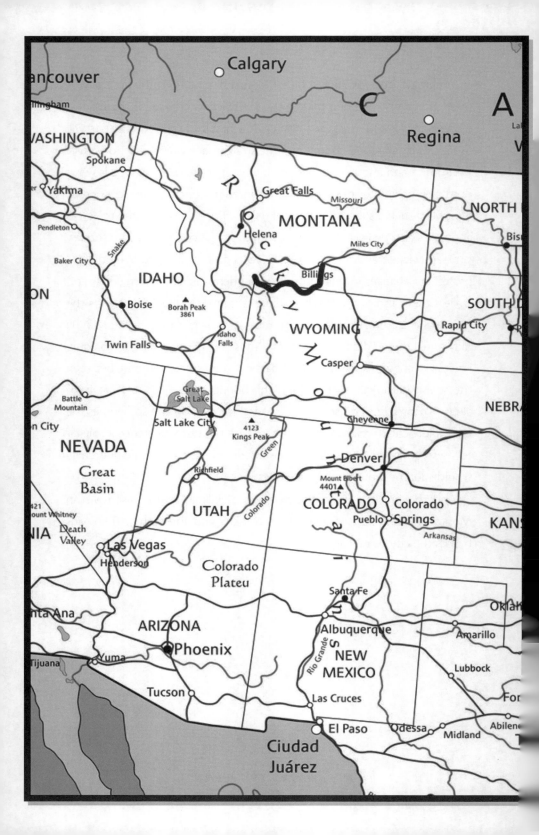

Chapter Seven

BILLINGS TO YELLOWSTONE

The proximity of Billings triggered a couple of thoughts. Firstly, this was the first 'real' city we had encountered since leaving St Paul/ Minneapolis. Although in the US, the nomenclature 'city' is used loosely as it often relates back to pioneering times, we've been brought up with different parameters. To us a city has to have a population in excess of 20,000 or a cathedral. Those with cathedrals but insufficient population are known as cathedral cities and are very few. Not for us a Mound City with 65 people. Billings has about 100,000 people and is where originally John Sutherland was going to have Sylvia fly to as he thought the ride would be too difficult and she wouldn't be up to the discomfort of it. This brought forth protest from both Sylvia and Pirsig. What Pirsig wrote about this is so much in line with how I feel that I wanted to shout "Yes, yes!" when I read it.

> … *physical discomfort is important only when the mood is wrong. Then you fasten on to whatever thing is uncomfortable and call that the cause. But if the mood is right, then physical discomfort doesn't mean much. And when thinking about Sylvia's moods and feelings, I couldn't see her complaining.*
>
> *Also, to arrive in the Rocky Mountains by plane would be to see them*

in one kind of context, as pretty scenery. But to arrive after days of hard travel across the prairies would be to see them in another way, as a goal, a promised land. If John and I and Chris arrived with this feeling and Sylvia arrived seeing them as 'nice' and 'pretty', there would be more disharmony among us than we would get in the heat and monotony of the Dakotas.

I've always felt that attainment through struggle is always so much sweeter. I feel for the children of the rich who want for nothing, can buy pleasures both physical and material at the click of a finger. I can't see them ever getting the same enjoyment from a bicycle that an after-school job has paid for or the exhilaration of the beginning of a journey after months of deprivation. It is also the responsibility of choice that concerns me. If there is no struggle, there is no responsibility of choice when that decision is called for. When there is a struggle, the moment of choice is one of excited trepidation because of the importance of getting it right. The attainment will always be something to savour with pride. To be able to buy without concern and reject without concern is not something to envy.

It had developed into another hard day and we were pleased to reach Laurel and the Russell Motel. Surprisingly it was pink but homely and our unit may have been old but it was bigger than we'd become used to. It had three bedrooms and a separate lounge and kitchen and a TV. Laurel was typical of a flat inland town but interesting all the same for us. Kitty and I explored some back streets and lanes on foot. It was so ordinary, so unglamorous that it sort of appealed in a perverse way. We found the obligatory beer shop. Each day needed to be celebrated with a small reward of the nectar of the gods ... and Myles needed it to help him sleep. The ubiquitous Subway provided the evening meal. This was the bonus of the town not being too tiny. Subway provided good choices of ingredients for 12-inch-long sandwich rolls. I had to make a small compromise by going there, but I have a good justification. I had long ago taken a personal stand against the multi-nationals, last entering a McDonalds in Panama City for a milkshake in 1977. My stand is against the unnatural global spread by the corporations. We can, and did make nice hamburgers in New Zealand before the arrival of McD's. We didn't need a formulaic pre-cooked hamburger in a cardboard box, but that is what we got, to the detriment of the small businesses that previously had produced nice made-to-order hamburgers. They all slowly went to the wall, because Head Office in the US would have given the word to establish an operation in New Zealand and … outlast the competition. They'd build their standard, clean, hygienic, new facilities and erect their Golden Arches for the benefit of … well not us. Subway has also reached us, and despite the nice, quite healthy food, I won't use them because we didn't need them, and if someone thought there was a need for something similar, well they could have made one themselves. Fortunately, I can live with US corporations having outlets all over the US, because that is where I have always said they should have stayed. And so it was with a clear conscience that I luxuriated, in scoffing a delicious Subway 'something-or-other', my first. Bloody lovely.

It was here at Laurel that Pirsig cheered up a bit because he was back in the presence of the mountains. He could see them and feel the cool breeze from them. He felt happy but a little sad too. "Sometimes it is a little better to travel than to arrive." Next morning, they were all happy, John was out walking and Sylvia and Chris chatted companionably about school and friends while Pirsig gazed out the window thinking back to South Dakota. Sylvia said to him that John had talked to someone in town and been told there was another way to Bozeman, south through Yellowstone Park.

"South?" I say. "You mean Red Lodge?"

"I guess so."

A memory comes back to me of snowfields in June. "That road goes way up above the timberline."

"Is that bad?" Sylvia asks.

"It'll be cold." In the middle of the snowfields in my mind appear the cycles

and us riding on them. "But just tremendous."

Finally, we would be leaving the plains and prairies. There would be corners, there would be curves, there would be dips and hollows, there would be vistas – all the things that motorcyclists love. The view would be ever-changing, and so would be the road. Now, there'd be concentration and excitement, the challenge of putting the bike where you want it, when you want it, on the twisty road to the sky. We wouldn't be what the English call 'earholing' it, as our bikes were laden but there was still a lot of pleasure to be gained by accurately and smoothly making the old girls dance. This would be more of a waltz than a samba –still fun and enjoyable when done well. It was this day, high on the Beartooth Pass, that the photo that changed my dreaming into this *Zen* ride was taken. There was an eagerness that you could almost taste. We knew it had the potential to be cold, hey they told us that, but going over a 11,000 ft pass would always be cold. This was a mountain road that was only warm enough to be open for a couple months of the year.

Just as they did, we followed the twisting blacktop up a valley in bright morning sunlight, dipping into the cold shady areas more often than we'd like. It was interesting without being spectacular, but that was good because this was just the entree. It would be awful to climax too soon … we hadn't even had breakfast yet. It was only an hour and a half to Red Lodge, all of it spent climbing gently, hardly knowing you're doing it. Like Pirsig, we were shivering when we reached the little alpine town that is Red Lodge. Now touristy, quaint in a little twee fashion, it was still a surprise to us. Nestled against the mountains at 5,500 ft, it was very unlike the towns on the flatlands. It really was alpine in its presentation, not quite Switzerland, but a good local interpretation of what an alpine town should look like. Despite not seeing any on the road, the main street was already filled with motorcycles. We were not the only ones afoot this day.

A good stack of pancakes was called for, good hot doughy pancakes with sweet syrup. This was an excellent way to warm up before facing the pass. The diner chosen was mainly patronised by motorcyclists, some going off to do the loop – over the pass into Wyoming through Cody City and around again, just for pleasure. Word in the diner was that it is 31 degrees at the top. On our scale, that is below zero. This didn't make us try and rush our food, we were happy to let the sun do its work. We lingered outside and chat to some motorcyclists from Egypt. They'd flown over, hired Harleys and were having the time of their lives. We lingered on the sunny side of the main street. The shops were selling upmarket, artsy-crafty stuff aimed at a clientele that we would never be. It was also unlike the 'normal' towns, the working towns. This was a resort town … adventure was in the air. This was a gateway for skiing, climbing, mountain-biking and hiking. We half-heartedly looked in one classy shop but weren't made welcome. That was fair enough, as we'd never be serious customers. It was warmer outside and time to go.

Soon the broadleaf deciduous trees no longer dominated the landscape, being replaced by the darker, more foreboding conifers. These pine trees were often just in small clumps and clusters as we climber higher and higher. The road curved and climbed in swoops for a while before starting to become switchbacks with rugged bluffs soaring steeply from the road edge. Climbing opened up more and more views of spectacular mountainous countryside. We did a couple of filmed 'ride pasts'. With the road is as good as this, it was no chore to drop Kitty off and go back down away from her, then in formation ride back up and past. Intermittently, we passed other motorcyclists also carving their way through the day. Those without helmets were seen to be grinning, even in the cool air. The road got a lot of attention from contractors because of the difficulty in keeping it open. It was almost a constant battle against rockfalls and landslides. Today, it was great, the contractors working but not intrusive. They waved us through good-naturedly. We were now being faced with a spectacular renewal of the view at every corner. We were looking for Rock Creek Vista where we think 'our' photo was taken. We could tell it was a bit of a layby from the photo and Pirsig called it a 'turnout'. Finally, we came across a suitable candidate. We stopped and got out the battered Manila file which contained all our Zen info. This looked like it ... maybe a bit wider, a bit further to the barriers in their shot, but we were able to line up the far-off glaciers and peaks. It wasn't as snow-clad today but it would do ... and we hadn't found anywhere else that fitted the bill. A Dutch family were at the same place and were press-ganged into doing the photographing. We showed them the photo we wanted to recreate. Myles put his hand in his jacket, just like young Chris. Kitty and I put ours around each other's shoulders, as John and Sylvia did. It felt good. This is why we were there.

It was not a long stop. We did our thing, then moved on. We had all our thermals on, so we warmed a little in the sun before making a run for the top. Soon there were no more trees at all. There was quite a flat zone at the top of the pass. There was a false top, an almost summit and a nice ride along an open, tawny, grassy landscape, laced with the little wild flowers I'd read that we would see. Finally, it was the top and we were saying goodbye to a panorama of strong mountains and jagged peaks with deep valleys and ravines. Pirsig summed it up well with his thoughts:

I look over my shoulder for one last view of the gorge. Like looking down to the bottom of the ocean. People spend their entire lives at those lower altitudes without any awareness that this high country exists.

For one who often takes pages and pages to analyse classic thoughts and objects, his romantic utterings are often very concise and for me accurate and emotive. I love the 'roadtrip' words so much. They may be shallow and facile ... I don't know, for I always find them descriptive and inspiring.

We rode up to a view point and stopped. Ahead was a different and bigger view. Below us lay Wyoming. We could almost see forever. There were numerous lakes and buttes of all sizes and it really was like the

BILLINGS TO YELLOWSTONE
155

archetypical 'rumpled sheet' landscape that travel writers portray, but a bit more flattened out. We were far, far above it and could see the road twisting and winding away down from the summit. We could see possibly a hundred turns. It was like the twirling ribbon of an Olympic gymnast had been frozen in motion, then just laid out across the disappearing land. It oozed fun potential, but it was something to be savoured. We would rest first.

Fortunately, it was now warmer than the 31 degrees promised back in Red Lodge. It was not unpleasant whilst still clad like the Michelin Man, and we walked around and explored a little. I explored a little further, unsuccessfully looking for the marmots said to be found in the rocky clefts, while Myles and Kitty decided on a rest. I returned to find Myles flat on his back, helmet still on, snoozing in the sun, fingers laced together over his tum, ankles delicately crossed ... contented. It was time to re-

enter this 'biscuit tin lid' landscape, and to my surprise, I watched Myles decline the track back to the road ... and just ride straight ahead, bumping cross-country, sidling across the tussocky slope, taking his own way down, a short-cut. My on-camera comment to Kitty was, "I can't believe he is really going down there, is he?" Kitty eagerly called back, "Quick, quick, I've got to film him if he does!" We followed cautiously, knowing this could all end in tears or more likely a drop to the road below that we couldn't ... drop. This straight-down approach cut off a big loop-around and fortunately we both did find a spot that we were happy enough to let gravity help us with. It was not quite an 'eyes shut' moment but rather a 'hold your breath' one as we dropped back onto the seal. Again, we did a bit of filming with Kitty positioned to record us riding away down the road, then doubling back ... facing her but dropping away, a level lower. Bikes passed companionably with a wave. We knew we were sharing a

special ride, one that some US motorcyclists rate as being the best on the continent. We enjoyably dropped to a wide valley floor, now back among trees and lakes. We paused for a brew beside a lake under the shadow of an enormous butte.

This was Clay Butte in Shoshone National Park, and it soared above us to a height of almost 10,000 ft. There was a fire lookout at its top, but we didn't have the time or spirit for a major detour. The Thermette soon had our water boiling and a welcome and warming brew resulted ... yet again to be eagerly cradled in cupped hands. A deer appeared in the thin bushland opposite, wandering among the saplings unperturbed by our presence. It is no more than 20 yards away and I immediately thought of my old *Last Hurrah* riding partner Dick. Dick is a hunter ... one who has hunted deer professionally in New Zealand, making his living doing it and providing for his family of five kids. I recalled his tales of long tramps in unfriendly bush-clad hills, seeking out the very same as was watching us

now. Her ears were up and alert, but she wasn't afraid, probably knowing she had the speed and skill to get away from us. In New Zealand, deer have been hunted for both sport and also in areas and times of need, the government has put a bounty on them because of the damage they do to the natural flora and fauna. Dick had been one of these 'cullers' for a period, bringing in sacks of ears for payment, after extended periods away in the wild. It was so unfamiliar to see one so close. Of course, we were later to learn they even come into the gardens of urban California. But for us now, the thrill warranted a couple of photos.

As always we rode on, to us it was just another working day. We'd just had a late morning tea, that's all. We wouldn't be having our weekend for a couple more days yet. As we dropped in altitude, our bodies warmed to match our spirits. We paused for Myles to check his plugs as he felt that all performance had dropped away, but I thought we had been going uphill. All seemed well so we pressed on, now back among the trees. We reached another roadworks collection point, pulling up behind six or so Harley Davidsons, all Michigan registered. The riders were middle-aged and wearing the durag rather than helmets. We all note with a smile, that one of them was riding in what looks like bed slippers. They came over for a chat and once they spotted our plates, they were loquacious and friendly, sharing what I would never share. They asked how we got here and our answers, reflected the truth. It turned out that they have had one of their number, drive some sort of big vehicle from Michigan towing a trailer with all their bikes on or in it. The rest of them had then flown in and reconnected to 'ride the twisties'. I suppressed my thoughts of anger, it was their lives and not everyone feels there must be struggle before reward. It did just seem so wrong though, and something I could never bring myself to do. It is not quite on the same scale as having a helicopter take you to the top of Mt Everest but it is the beginning of the sort of philosophy that leads to taking the pleasures 'because you can'. If you're going for the view, the end result is the same it could be argued. "Who needs the pain?" We'd become used to the ridiculous in the US and only shared this slightly bizarre behaviour later, revelling in the unsuitability of it. Where we come from, you'd never own up to it. Pride would stop you doing it anyway. It would be like wearing a toupée. You're always going to be the butt of jokes behind your back.

Whilst I was cogitating on whether to comment on their 'wussiness' or to meekly acquiesce with "what a good idea!", a huge bug with long antennae landed on me. It was enormous and we were thrilled by its appearance and started to film it. The lollipop lady cames over and told us it is a plain beetle, a horrible tree-eating monster that was almost single-handedly destroying the forests. I never did comment on the softness of the other riders. They were having fun in a matey way, probably thinking

that they were the Road Warriors from Hell.

Our time in Wyoming ass only fleeting, and our route soon took us back into Montana and down the Beartooth All American Road to Cooke. This was quite unlike Red Lodge, yet would be a rival adventure centre, being the other side of the same range. It seemed younger-focused somehow. It was still alpine, but the main street was wider, the surrounding country a flat buffer before the forested hills. It was here that Pirsig notes that John and Sylvia looked and sounded happier than he had seen them for years. They'd enjoyed hot beef sandwiches and were pleased to be a bit warmer even though rain was threatening. Pirsig knew he was often remote and felt that Chris was the one who understands why. He commented:

> I suppose if I were a novelist rather than a Chautauqua orator I'd try to 'develop the characters' of John and Sylvia and Chris with action-packed scenes that would reveal 'inner meanings' of Zen and maybe Art and maybe even Motorcycle Maintenance. That would be quite a novel, but for some reason I don't feel quite up to it. They're friends not characters, and as Sylvia herself once said, "I don't like being an object!" So a lot of things we know about one another I'm simply not going into. Nothing bad, but not really relevant to the Chautauqua. That's the way it should be with friends.
>
> At the same time I think you can understand from the Chautauqua why I must always seem so reserved and remote to them. Once in a while they ask questions that seem to call for a statement of what the hell I'm always thinking about, say, the 'a priori' presumption of the continuity of a motorcycle from second to second and do this without benefit of the entire edifice of the Chautauqua, they'd just be startled and wonder what is wrong. I really am interested in this continuity and the way we talk and think about it and so tend to get removed from the usual lunchtime situation and this gives an appearance of remoteness. It's a problem.

It was a problem, and Pirsig finally twigged to the fact that young Chris was like a barometer. He reflected the mood of the moment, happy when Pirsig was relaxed and in a good mood, but nervous and anxious when he sensed his father's troubles were upon him. Chris tried to keep him from those troubles and answered some of the questions from the Sutherlands about the people they are going to stay with in Bozeman ... even though the questions had been addressed to Pirsig. It was obvious that approaching Bozeman was difficult, as memories kept intruding. In some ways Bozeman had been both the zenith and nadir of Pirsig's life. They were going to stay with the De Weese family. De Weese had been a work colleague of Pirsig's at the college there. He now worried about how much De Weese would be thinking he would remember of their times together. Pirsig was now vague about his time in Bozeman, only remembering snatches through Phaedrus. He thought they were friends even though De Weese was an art teacher and Phaedrus an engineering-focussed philosophy professor. They were opposites in thinking, each confused as to the way the other thought and comprehended things. One the romantic thinker, the other the classic.

I like De Weese because of his perceptions and grounded wisdom. A couple of examples come through in the book. Pirsig recalls Phaedrus being disappointed in the realisation that the students he liked best were the ones most like him in outlook. De Weese agrees and reassures him that is quite normal. Phaedrus complains, though, that he doesn't understand it as these are the students with the worst grades. De Weese laughs at these concerns telling him that the best students are always flunking. "Every good teacher knows that!" Phaedrus feels that De Weese's enigmatic responses often come from a hidden resource of understanding, one that he doesn't comprehend. He seems quick and wise. On another occasion Phaedrus has fixed a technical problem and De Wees exclaims:

"How do you know all that?"

"It's obvious."

"Well then why didn't I see it?"

"You have to have some familiarity."

"Then it is not obvious then, is it?"

I wonder if I like De Weese, because he liked Pirsig or if I like him because I can identify with his romantic understanding. I feel an easy fraternal companionship with romantic thoughts but no connection with classic analysis to the intense level that Pirsig takes it.

We dallied long enough in Cooke City to send some emails from the gas station, which has a facility to do so included in its premises. We were soon aiming for Yellowstone Park, all of us humming "Dumpty doo". We needed to cut through the park to get to our overnight stop at Gardiner, which is the north entry. We'd come in through the north-east entrance and only have a 50 mile ride through Americas oldest National Park. The ride is coolish and interesting enough … if you hadn't just ridden over Beartooth Pass. Our gate experience was somehow like theirs nearly 40 years earlier. I include the passage from ZAMM because it says it well:

'At the park entrance we stop and pay a man in a Smokey Bear hat. He hands us a one-day pass in return. Ahead I see an elderly tourist take a movie of us, then smile. From under his shorts protrude white legs into street stockings and shoes. His wife who watches approvingly has identical legs. I wave to them as we go by and they wave back. It's a moment that will be preserved on film for years.

Phaedrus despised this park without knowing exactly why – because he hadn't discovered it himself, perhaps, but probably not. Something else. The guided-tour attitude of the rangers angered him. The Bronx Zoo attitudes of the tourists disgusted him even more. It seemed an enormous museum with exhibits carefully manicured to give the illusion of reality, but nicely chained off so that children would not injure them. People enter the park and become polite and cozy and fakey to each other because the atmosphere of the park made them that way. In the entire time he had lived within a hundred miles of it he had visited it only once or twice.'

For us, it was a female Smokey-Bear-hatted guide. The pass was quite expensive especially as we wouldn't be exploring the park to any great extent but that is not their fault. The ride through was nice, with bison grazing away in the middle distance. It was a little like Pirsig recorded, and I felt a sense of guilt. This wasn't something you should criticise. This enormous park has been established in a natural wonderland, and geysers and hot pools abound. There are wolves in the hills, grizzly bears even. This was established back in 1872 with great foresight. It just seemed a little 'too' right and the slow-moving tourists animal-watching seemed to detract somehow. I kept my thoughts to myself as it is a bit like wanting to run over Bambi ... you suppress the urge for fear of being publicly reviled. The afternoon was running away from us, and the day had been long and

varied … we needed completion and shelter. A short stop was taken at Mammoth where there were touristy hot springs and deer nibbling away on the lawns of the civic buildings. Possibly, these are the most photographed deer on the planet. Dick and his 303 would soon take the smug looks off their faces I thought, as we used the toilet facilities, then moved on again. This constant need to move on, was one of the downsides to our travelling, one that we lived with uncomplainingly.

The large Roosevelt Arch defines the north entrance, the cornerstone of which was laid by Teddy himself. This is the only open-all-year way into the park. It is impressive and a nice indicator that our day was almost done. Gardiner is just outside the park, is tiny (pop. 900) and clings to the steep sides of the Yellowstone River. It was touristy and frontier-townish at the same time, yet didn't have the crass neon feel that many US places of renown have. It was cold now because we were still in the mountains and still about a mile above sea level. It was crisp when the sun fell. We found

the motel straight across the bridge, just like Pirsig described, and we saw the neat little cabins he was so enthused about. This was another satisfying moment because we weren't guessing … we knew they stayed here. Astonishingly, they were all full, and much as the proprietors would have liked us to have that special night with the ghosts of times past, it was not to be. Before we left Myles had a look at the cabins that Pirsig so praised for the workmanship. Pirsig had admired the double-hung sash windows and how well everything had been made. Myles immediately spotted that the cover boards on the windows had been constructed contrary to good carpentry practice. Many think that the head member, the one that goes over the top of the window should be continued right across and the side cover boards butted up to it. This is how these windows had been done. It is not the right way, as the side cover boards should go all the way up with the top member cut between. The cover flashing then protects the end grain of the side cover boards, and this is better construction. Pirsig's classic understanding should have been able to work that out.

Fortunately, up around the corner was another camp almost perched on the side of the high river bank. We gratefully took up the offer of a tiny cabin, one of two down a dirt track below the office and ablution block. We had a set-back when Kitty dropped her glasses in the office and broke the frame. She would have to stay half-blind for a day or so until we reached Bozeman. Fortunately, we were only a couple of hours away from this goal.

In the twilight, we saw a large deer or possibly an elk or even the biggest of all, the moose, wandering slowly through the yards of the houses opposite on the other side of the river. It wasn't furtive, it just seemed a little cautious, yet also familiar with the urban surroundings. We walked down to the shops on our side of the river and find a Subway. I was becoming a regular almost. They were nice, and I should savour while I could. Our first impressions held. It was a tourist town but almost quite classy and subtle, something we hadn't seen much of. It even has a second-hand book shop in a cafe. Myles decided that the opportunity to sleep outside on the little veranda that faced the river and the beautiful hills beyond, was something he would take advantage of and despite the impending cold night, he moved his sleeping pad so he could watch the night sky and later greet the dawn.

Before retiring, we did a bit of reading of the handouts from the female ranger back at the park entrance. There was so much to absorb, that it was a little overwhelming. Of interest to us was the amount of matter relating to what you can't do, shouldn't do and mustn't do. The bear section gave us entertainment enough to be worth the quite expensive price of entry for the period we needed. We learned that those cuddly-looking animals we've seen in zoos waddling around their enclosures and flopping into fetid pools are actually super-athletes. They can run faster than us over a short distance, easily outswim us and climb trees way, way quicker than us. I don't totally believe this, as they probably haven't timed people being chased by a bear to see how fast they can run, swim and climb. When faced by a huge animal that can traverse across the surface of the planet faster than you can, I wonder how the 'fight or flight' decision making would go. Neither seems a good option at first visit. Our little guidebook didn't really tell us what to do. What it did explain, though, was that they don't want bears to learn that humans are a source of easy food. They don't want you to see a bear and throw off your pack and run away as fast as your little frightened legs and sticky pants will allow. What that would do, they say, is give bears the idea that, to get food, all they have to do is find a human with a pack and go "Grrrrraaaahh!!!" and the human will give up the goods. What they want you to do is keep your pack on but still get away as fast as you can. Hello!!! ... you're going to need every ounce of speed for the run of your life ... this is more than the Olympic final of the 200 m, and they want you to keep your pack on your back for a bit of a handicap. Logic would tell you that, with the bear already being rated as faster than you, maybe the bear should be wearing the pack and some leg-

irons as well. Surely you don't handicap the slower athlete! When told of all this Myles responded with his gruff voice. "Be fucked if I'm going to keep my pack on just to save the fat arse of some future American." We all resolved that this wasn't one park rule we'd be sticking to.

Snug inside our little timber cabin next morning, I heard the muted mumbling sounds of Myles talking to

the motorcyclists who have moved in next door to the matching cabin. I thought one of them had also slept on the veranda. I could smell the thermette devouring more leaves and twigs. Today on his coffee round, Myles had included our neighbours who turned out to be a pleasant foursome from West Virginia. All young and attractive, they were on Harleys of course and were a little in awe of our simple little bikes, and in particular the Thermette. They took photos of it and of us and our bikes. I photographed them photographing us. They were wearing the uniform of the US bikers who do actually ride the highways. They wear fringed leather chaps, which have never made sense to us. Yes, they mirror the romantic past of the wild west in cowboy tradition, but what do they do? Having your crotch not covered means they don't keep you warm all over, and if the idea is to not have your privates protected for cooling purposes, I would have thought that to not wear them at all would be more successful. I do have to concede that they would provide impact and abrasion protection, as your groin isn't usually the first point of impact in the event of an unfortunate spill. I still think they are more show than go, and I find it ironic that increasingly in New Zealand we are also adopting the HOG culture, and chaps are appearing even though our stockmen never wore such an item. So for us, it isn't reflecting our past. It is yet again an example of just mimicking popular celebrity culture. I've heard anecdotal tales back home of women saying that they have been pressured into wearing them by their menfolk because they look so sexy. Each to their own, and again I know Steph would give me short shrift if I suggested such an item for her to disport herself in.

Myles wanted to do a bit of service work on the Honda first up, so Kitty and I went back into Yellowstone for the morning. We did the touristy thing with the limestone cascades at Mammoth. They're nice and worth the walk up the conveniently provided walkways. A scenic spot is always better if there is a walk to it. If you can just drive your car to a waterfall and

look out the window, it is not as good as one you have had to walk for an hour to get to, to see. It is that pleasure of attainment as a result of struggle ... does it every time. I noticed a couple of slightly different Harleys in the carpark. They were laden, had screens and panniers, reasonably capacious petrol tanks and numerous rally stickers on them showing they really had been ridden all over the US and Canada. They were Police models, a few years old and looked quite equal to the tasks they had endured. I could almost see myself on one. We'd been told of a spot where there is a confluence of a stream resulting from a hot spring and the main river itself. It was not on any of the guide material that we had been provided with by the ranger, nor was it sign-posted ... it was just known about. It was called Boiling River and was only a half mile or so walk from one of the main through routes. A few people passed us on their way out, hair wet, carrying towels, which was a good sign we were on the right path.

When we did reach the spot there were a couple of women wriggling their way out of swimming gear and into their clothes whilst wrapped in towels to preserve their modesty. They were mainly successful in this, and whilst we disrobed discreetly, giving them space, we couldn't help but overhear a few snippets of their chat. Our flapping ears picked that their accents were so normal that they could be 'one of us' ... they were. When you are from a country as small as New Zealand, it is always nice to have an interaction with other Kiwis when you encounter them in nice far-away places. This was no exception. It is funny that I am happy to meet my fellow countrymen in a place like this ... out in the open countryside, in a place of natural beauty, mostly unclad and feeling exposed, yet in Venice's St Mark's Square, I would have ignored them totally. It is something about tourists versus travellers. Maybe the remoteness of the location contains

certain knowledge of that journey to attainment, I don't know really. After a brief but pleasurable interlude, they soon slipped away, and Kitty and I slid into the warm water in our undies, happy to be left alone to enjoy the unique experience. The temperature was controlled by where you sat. You could choose really hot or just warm or even damn cold by moving only a matter of a couple of yards. The hot spots did move a little from time to time but not much and it was a pleasant time to just soak away any tensions. We chatted easily, both half blind with no glasses on in the steamy pool.

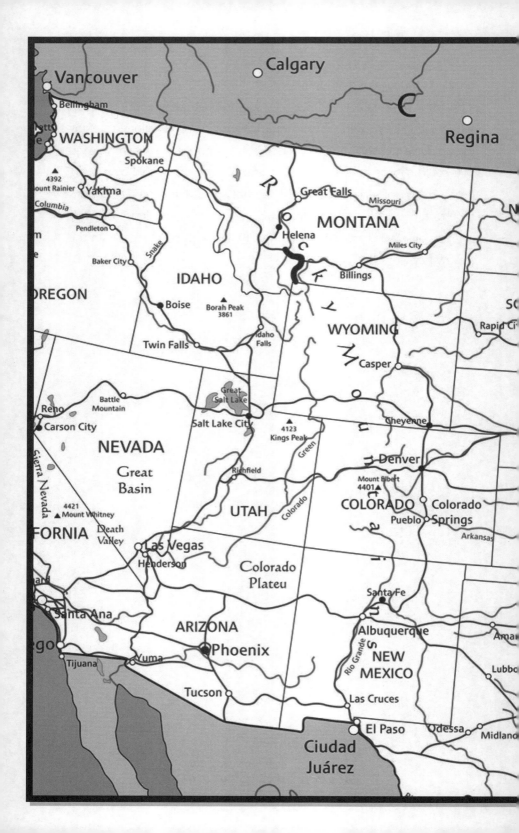

Chapter Eight

BOZEMAN

All too soon it was lunchtime and time to get under way. We snacked in Gardiner before heading off to Livingston, where we would turn west for the last 20 miles or so to Bozeman. For Pirsig, this was a crucial day … he struggled to get his food down, whilst the Sutherlands were still filled with the joy of yesterday. Pirsig was daunted by the prospect of the arrival back into the physicality of his past.

I really don't want to go back there. I'd just as soon turn around and go back. Just tension, I guess.

It fits one of the fragments of this memory, in which many mornings the tension was so intense he would throw up everything before he got to his first classroom. He loathed appearing before classrooms of students and talking. It was a complete violation of his whole lone, isolated way of life, and what he experienced was intense stage fright, except that it never showed on him as stage fright, but rather as a terrible intensity in everything he did. Students had told his wife it was just like electricity in the air. The moment he entered the classroom, all eyes turned on him and followed him as he walked to the front of the room. All conversation died to a hush and remained at a hush, even though it was several minutes, often, before the class started. Throughout the hour the eyes never strayed from him.

There was more to Pirsig's fear than just a recollection of possible past inadequacies. There were obviously things going on that he really struggled with on a human level and a 'belief' level. He noted that the college was a 'teaching college', one that does no research … it just teaches. He felt that this was just a way of having a college on the cheap. He didn't seem to have been an enthusiastic supporter of their scholastic regime and, he recalled his 'Church of Reason' lecture that seems to have really instigated the problems he would later endure. It is these sorts of recollections that of course elevate ZAMM from being a travel or adventure book. I've presented the next piece because not only do I understand it and agree with it but also because it helps to further explain the background fear Pirsig had about his return nearly a decade after his departure. He'd dared to put his head above the ramparts. It is also included because our journey was always more than just our journey. 'They' were never far away in spirit.

The state of Montana at this time was undergoing an outbreak of ultra-right-wing politics like that which occurred in Dallas, Texas, just prior to President Kennedy's assassination. A nationally known professor from the University of Montana at Missoula, was prohibited from speaking on campus on the grounds that it would 'stir up trouble.' Professors were told that all public statements must be cleared through the college public-relations office before they could be made.

Academic standards were demolished. The legislature had previously prohibited the school from refusing entry to any student over twenty-one whether he had a high-school diploma or not. Now the legislature had passed a law fining the college eight thousand dollars for every student who failed, virtually an order to pass every student.

The newly elected governor was trying to fire the college president for both personal and political reasons. The college president was not only a personal enemy, he was a Democrat, and the governor was no ordinary Republican. His campaign manager doubled as state co-ordinator for the John Birch Society. This was the same governor who supplied the list of fifty subversives we heard about a few days ago.

Now, as part of this vendetta, funds to the college were being cut. The college president had passed on unusually large part of the cut to the English department, of which Phaedrus was a member, and whose members had been quite vocal on issues of academic freedom.

Phaedrus had given up, was exchanging letters with the Northwest Regional Accrediting to see if they could help prevent these violations of accreditation requirements. In addition to this private correspondence he had publicly called for an investigation of the entire school situation. At this point some students in one of his classes has asked Phaedrus, bitterly, if his efforts to stop accreditation meant he was trying to prevent them from getting an education.

Phaedrus said no.

Then one student, apparently a partisan of the governor, said angrily that the legislature would prevent the school from losing its accreditation.

Phaedrus asked how.

The student said they would post police to prevent it.

Phaedrus pondered this for a while, then realized the enormity of the student's misconception of what accreditation was all about.

That night, for the next day's lecture, he wrote out his defence of what he was doing. This was the Church of Reason lecture, which, in contrast to his usual sketchy lecture notes, was very long and very carefully elaborated.

It begins with references to a newspaper article about a country church building with an electric beer sign hanging right over the front entrance. The building had been sold and was being used as a bar. One can guess that some classroom laughter started at this point. The college was well-known for drunken partying and the image vaguely fit. The article said a number of people had complained to the church officials about it. It had been a Catholic church, and the priest who had been delegated to respond to the criticism, had sounded quite irritated about the whole thing. To him it had revealed an incredible ignorance of what a church really was. Did they think that bricks and boards and glass constituted a church? Or the shape of the roof? Here, posing as piety was an example of the very materialism the church opposed. The building in question was not holy ground. It had been de-sanctified. That was the end of it. The beer sign resided over a bar not a church, and those who couldn't tell the difference were simply revealing something about themselves.

Phaedrus said the same confusion existed about the University and that was why the loss of accreditation was hard to understand. The real University is not a material object. It is not a group of buildings that can be defended by police. He explained that when a college lost its accreditation, nobody came and shut down the school. There were no legal penalties, no fines, no jail sentences. Classes did not stop. Everything went on just as before. Students got the same education they would have if the school didn't lose its accreditation. All that would happen, Phaedrus said, would simply be an official recognition of a condition that already existed. It would be similar to excommunication. What would happen is that the 'real' University, which no legislature can dictate to and which can never be identified by any location of bricks or boards or glass, would simply declare that this place was no longer 'holy ground'. The real University would vanish from it and all that would be left was the bricks and the books and the material manifestation.

It must have been a strange concept to all of the students, and I can imagine him waiting for a long time for it to sink in, and perhaps then waiting for the question, What do you think the real University is?

His notes, in response to this question, state the following:

The real University, he said, has no specific location. It owns no property, pays no salaries and receives no material dues. The real University is a state of mind.

And so we passed by banks of sage brush and finally rolled into Bozeman. Somehow, it seemed so good. We arrived in the centre of town quite easily and without passing a single strip mall. There were older brick buildings, interesting-looking cafes and book shops, there were people riding bicycles, there are footpaths with people bustling about, there are antique shops. It was a proper city centre – full of life and colour. You could sense that it is a university town but more … it was an adventure town. The hills and rivers were not far away. Kitty and I found an optician while Myles explored. After a good look at the problem, the helpful proprietor referred us on to a jeweller, who she felt had better equipment for making a repair. The jeweller's was a very classy place. They were not just resellers of items from a wholesaler's catalogue, they also manufactured their own stuff. I do not usually patronise shops like this. If you want to feel insecure or out of your depth, go into a shop like this. This shop would not have disgraced London's Hatton Garden area. In our quite dowdy roadgear, we didn't meet the profile of their normal clientele. The dapper, besuited artisan who was directed to solve our problem, couldn't have been more helpful. He said he could use a laser welder to fuse the two parts of the frame back together in a far superior way than trying to solder it. In 15 minutes, we were done, and soon we were snacking away contentedly in the best eatery so far. We'd spotted a food co-op that was just loaded with organic produce, and our hearts pounded a little faster when we spot Weleda health products from Havelock North, New Zealand, on the shelves. If a town had a shop as good as this, it had to be good.

We needed a camp where we can base ourselves for a couple of days. We had lots of things to do while we were here. Myles had decided that the little Honda should be sold at the end of the journey. Whilst it was comfortable and seemingly reliable, he feels he hadn't bonded with it sufficiently to want to go through the costly exercise of repatriating it home. The plan was to list it on eBay now, and by the time we got to San Francisco, we could have a buyer. Replete food-wise and pleased with the day so far, we asked directions to a camp, thought we understood them, and headed off in the late afternoon. We didn't think we had far to go, as the camp mentioned seemed to be not far away, which made sense ... at the time. Hardly had we left the town limits when the rain came, big and wet, a cooling relief to a hot afternoon. Soon we were embroiled in riding in the darkening gloom with an electric storm breaking over us. Forked lightning speared to the ground directly ahead of us, looking like it would have hit the earth just over the next rise, exactly where the road we were following, was going. This was a little frightening, as in New Zealand, all the lightning we seem to get is sheet lightning, which lights up the sky and gives rise to huge thunder claps but doesn't go flashing down to earth like a devil's arrow. I couldn't remember having seen it before and certainly was daunted and decided not to go over the rise, pulling in to a farmhouse for respite and further advice. Luckily, we had gone too far and we were sent back towards town, away from Lucifer's fire show.

We located a KOA (Kamps of America!) camp, and Myles recalled the multitude of KOA camps he and Sandy used as they made their way across the continent 20 years earlier. We got a small standard log cabin. It enabled us to shed our sodden clothing, quickly turning the place into something resembling a Chinese laundry. The cabin was sturdy and simple. The door hinges were just timber dowel pivots, latching by a lever and linked cord. Nothing fancy and quite old-world looking. KOA are a bit formulaic but not too rule driven or oppressive towards us casual stoppers. I found it interesting to wander around because an Air Stream tour was staying for a couple of nights. I'd

first seen an Air Stream caravan in 1974 in Iran, marvelling at the sleek polished aluminium body and tapered ends. All our caravans were of fibreglass or plywood construction and looked home-built even when not, whilst this looked like an aircraft manufacturer had made it. Even now over 30 years later, they still looked good and a refreshing change from all the Winnebago-type motor-homes on the road. I did spot among the caravans, or trailer-homes as I think they may be called in the US, a self-driving Air Stream. Very clearly an Air Stream, it still had the polished aluminium body but had the four wheels at each corner rather than grouped in the middle, and of course the steering wheel was a bit of a giveaway.

On our day off, Myles polished the Honda and I photographed it for the eBay auction. We hoped people wouldn"t notice that the chain guard was not in place. Just like Pirsig's did in 1968, the bike had fractured the securing bracket, although his wasn't to do it for a couple of days yet … and then he got it fixed. We had just strapped it on with the luggage. The little Honda had done well, especially when you consider we weren't involved in the preparation and there hadn't been time for very good shake-down rides before we set off. Myles had to tinker a bit to get the running mixture right, but other than that and the speedo drive coming adrift, she had been a great little bike. Initially, there had been a reluctance to change into first gear from neutral. To help with this, Myles had cobbled up a bit of chain to enable him to use his hand to yank on it at the same time as he tried to nudge it up with his foot. Fortunately, his technique improved and it wouldn't be sold with a bit of chain dangling from the handle bars. In the planning stages, I had been surprised at the negativity of the 'special interest' groups for both bikes. Both have a good following and good internet forums, but both were dismissive of our efforts. Mostly they thought the bikes to be too small, too old and not suited for a cross-continent ride. It was nice to be showing them what we knew all along … the bikes were made for this.

It was a shame that the Honda wouldn't be going home with the BMW but that was Myles's choice. Financially it wouldn't ever have really been an option unless he'd loved it to bits and couldn't bear to be parted from it ... and knowing Myles, I smile as I write this, he's not that kinda guy. The Super Hawk is collectible but not valuable enough to make it worthwhile doing, and we hoped that California would be a new home. Whilst I've not owned a Japanese motorcycle for myself, this was one I had coveted when a teenager. I'd even bought an LP of John Hammond, the blues singer, just because it had a picture of him in front of a New York cityscape, sitting on a red Honda Super Hawk. He and it looked so cool that I ordered the LP through the record club I was in at the time. I didn't know him or the blues. I think I vainly hoped that some of his cool would rub off on me through the mature ownership choice I was demonstrating. Elvis also rode one in an inane movie where he was a circus roadie, but that didn't move me at all ... no maturity demonstrated there. I reflect, too, how it is funny how life turns out. Firstly, I wanted the Honda, but I was too young and it was unattainable, then later wanted a Yamaha YDS3 250 in 1968, and yet when I did get to the bike shop with money to spend, I wavered when I noticed a two-year-old, second-hand ex-Police Triumph 650cc 'Saint'. Being undecided, I tossed a coin, which went the way of the British classic. 40 years later, I have yet to own a Japanese bike, and I've ridden across 50 or so countries on old British and European bikes. I laugh to think that a different landing of the coin could have meant a more 'normal' life.

Bozeman was a short yet enjoyable rest for us, whilst for the Chautauqua it was an interesting five days. This was the turn-back point for the Sutherlands and also a critical time for Pirsig. He returned to the college where he had taught and where he had many troubled times. He also started to introduce 'quality' into ZAMM. It came back to him how an old female teacher about to retire said to him, "I hope you are teaching quality to your students?", weeks later seeking further assurance that he was. Although he told her he was, he started to worry and fret, "what is quality?"

Soon the thought interrupted again. Quality? There was something irritating, even angering about that question? He thought about it, and then thought some more, and then looked out the window, and then thought about it some more. Quality?

Four hours later he still sat there with his feet on the window ledge and stared out into what had become a dark sky. The phone rang, and it was his wife calling to find out what had happened. He told her he would be home soon, but then forgot about this and everything else. It wasn't until three o'clock in the morning that he wearily confessed to himself that he didn't have a clue as to what Quality was, picked up his briefcase and headed home.

Apart from staying with the De Weese family and farewelling the Sutherlands, Pirsig and Chris headed into the hills for a hike together. This is great, something I love the thought of, and agree is an important thing to do for both parties. This would have been something that Chris would remember forever … a strenuous adventure with your dad is a cornerstone of that special father-son relationship. This part of the book is hard for the amateur. Bloody hell, the couple of days in the hills takes 71 pages. In there, are some thought-provoking passages on mind, matter and quality and how Phaedrus knows deep down that he has to interrelate the metaphysical trinity of subject, object and quality. There is also some good stuff on student rebellion in his classes and how he out-thinks his students. In my humble opinion, some of this deep analysis frustrates those of us who are finding the rest of the book exciting. We love the road trip and the relationships, we probably like the snippets from the past, Phaedrus has some good stuff to say, but the challenging explanations are tertiary institution academic stuff. It threatens to ruin a good adventure book … for some. We had not factored into our roadshow, the time to do his climb in the hills. This was a shame really, as I think it would have been a real highlight

We went to town, this time using an internet café to do our emailing. Kitty found a yoga book she had been looking for, while Myles bought his own copy of ZAMM. Here in a location central to the story, it seemed a little poignant. I photographed a couple of Schwinn Flying Star bicycles. We had nice coffee, nice bread rolls and a pecan slice. This was so far removed from the 'greasy spoons' we'd suffered on the back roads. We revelled in it, hardly able to contain our contentment. We liked this place. It was real, not ersatz, everything wasn't served in polystyrene buckets or little cardboard boxes by spotty teenagers. We suspected that somewhere was hidden the strip mall that I so hate, but it was not evident to us. I know I am not alone when I lament their coming. The 'curse of the Walmart' is so very central to the future of the US as the world's most powerful nation. New Zealand has never been a big manufacturer, and what we did make ourselves tended to be expensive and only viable because of import duties on the competition. We've slowly lost our own capability, but it hasn't had the impact that it will in the US, because it wasn't our core business, our heart. The US, however has always been a manufacturer ... of everything. The best cars were made here; the steel was renowned ... the most successful makers of all things. For Americans, everything your parents bought would have had 'Made in USA' stamped on it or not marked at all because it didn't need to be ... you knew it was home-built – there was nowhere else. A walk around a 1950s suburban home in any American small town would not have revealed any foreign-made items. But with the growth of the Walmart, all has changed. Founded in only 1962, it is the world's largest public corporation by revenue, it is the largest private employer in the world. That would be fine if the items being sold are, as The Boss sings "Born in the USA" ... but they're not. I know the shops provide employment and make cheap items available to eager buyers, but every branch has been built on the ashes of somebody else's dream. The local mom and pop stores that provided service for generations just went under the wrecking balls and bulldozers' blades. The proponents and supporters will say that you can't and shouldn't stop progress, but I don't see anything progressive about swamping the world with cheap mass-produced, low-quality goods. I am sure Phaedrus would agree with me.

We visited the food co-op again for supplies, and Kitty found a place to go to yoga that night. It was a relaxed little troop who headed back to camp, this time stopping at a half-derelict yard of dozens of old cars and trucks. These were haphazardly displayed with crude hand-painted signs giving prices. The range was inspiring, and I think of friends back home in the Early American Car Club. They'd be in clover. Here was a 1941 12-cylinder Lincoln, a 20s Dodge, numerous Plymouths and Chevys,

Oldsmobiles, a Fargo and even a European Tempo Matador van. None of the 60 or 70 vehicles there were restored and most looked undrivable, but they were 'starting points'. In the bike world, we call them basket cases. This was an interesting interlude, but it was back to camp to relax until yoga time. The cooking facilities for campers were small octagonal, open-sided hut-like constructions with benches right around on the inside, the cooking tops and sinks let into the work surface. The cook could work on the inside, and the diners congregated on the outside. When we went to our nearest one, a couple of young Czechs awee just finishing selling ice creams over the top to the young and old. We chatted, learning what it was like to work in the KOA network. There is a guide book for employees to seek summer work in the hundreds of camps across the country. It sounds fun, a good way to see the US. There are many older folk doing just this. Meanwhile, a nice meal of Spanish rice and frijoles resulted. Kitty enjoyed going to a formal yoga session but found it a bit simple. Just before I took her to town for this, we had a similar down-pour as the one we'd suffered the day before, but his time it hailed heavily. It had been a strange weather pattern that had hot days being ended so dramatically. It had been a good day but tomorrow we would hit the road early … we had got places to go, places to see, we still had a mission to fulfil.

I reflected on an interesting interlude from that morning. We'd been engaged in an easy conversation with a neighboring camper. He was temporarily living in the KOA because he had just shifted to town to run a tyre supply and repair franchise. We yarned companionably, sensing an affinity of thought. We looked upon ourselves as being guests in this big country, and had been very wary of voicing opinions regarding the Iraq war and the US involvement. Somehow in the conversation I mentioned my thoughts on Fox News, and how I felt they didn't present the news … they presented an opinion of the news. Our man laughed and told us of an instance in his last tyre shop when 10 or so customers were in the waiting room, reading magazines and chatting. One then mentioned something reasonably outrageous that Fox had presented the night before. "But you don't believe what Fox says", another responded to the group's laughter. It turned out that only one person in the room had any confidence that Fox told the news impartially.

America is a wonderfully diverse place. There are the enormous glass-towered cities, but there are still the homely little provincial towns dotted all over. Often what surprises visitors is the naivety and lack of worldliness of the ordinary man in the street. Of course, this shouldn't be a surprise, because by the time the TV news has covered the local issues and then the regional issues, the rest of the world gets only the barest mention. They also have a bred-in belief that they are the good guys and know that their fathers and grandfathers have made huge sacrifices for the good of the world. That has largely been true, but we all tend to think we are on the side of righteousness. On our roadshow we had been careful not to comment on or criticise the US efforts in world affairs, because this was very real for so many people. It wasn't just something you read about. These were real people who were going off in uniform, to serve as best they could. These were real family and friends who were spilling their blood on foreign soils ... real bravery, real hardship, real honour. We sensed also that there was not much knowledge about why.

We all tend to believe what we are told by our leaders. They stand before us, look us in the eye and sombrely tell us how it is. They're ours, made of the same history and values, so we listen and learn. So when the people who later became part of the 'coalition of the willing' were told how Iraq had weapons of mass destruction and were a huge world threat, the folk gasped and probably uttered things like "the bloody bastards!" Many of the subsequently non-involved around the world, of course, said "Fantastic, you're found them ... quick, tell Hans Blick. His UN Weapons Inspectors have been looking for them for 11 years. Finally, we've caught out Sadaam!" The UK were even told that the WMDs, as they had quickly been labelled, could be made to strike them in 20 minutes. When your leaders tell you this, it is persuasive, scary stuff. However, when the location of these WMDs couldn't or wouldn't be passed on to the on-the-ground independent inspectors, the outsiders ... the doubters, started to smell a rat. "You know where they are but can't tell ... do you really think I'd believe that?" So those of us whose leaders hadn't looked us in the eye and gravely said we've got to go to war to remove the world of this threat said "Bollocks!"

Time would show that there were no WMDs, the leaders would squirm and say they had been given poor intelligence advice. Those whose leaders they were meekly said, "Oh, that's OK then ... I suppose." To make it all right, the leaders shifted away from saying they had to remove the threat of WMDs and instead stressed the importance of "bringing democracy to the region" and that sadly in this case it was taking military force to do so. Most of the compliant citizens listening to these wisdoms had no idea of the importance of democracy in the region or otherwise. But they did know that their leaders wouldn't lie to them – not like some of those of foreign places. Surprisingly, they didn't seem eager to question the fact that the key launching points for military action, Pakistan and Saudi Arabia, are not democracies. They didn't seem confident to question and say, "If we're the shining knights bringing democracy to the world and it is important, why don't we start with some of the easy ones. Ones we can do with just one battleship and one helicopter. Why don't we do Fiji or Tonga, or the Himalayan Kingdom of Bhutan? ... we wouldn't even need a battleship for that one." They didn't point out that, for 10 years, the Marxist guerillas in Nepal had been fighting to get democracy while the US backed the inept royalty resisting it. The call for democracy was a smoke-shield. These same leaders had never called for it so stridently before, and not many asked "Why now?" And is it really that simple? What would happen if democracy was achieved by this military action and elections arranged and then from the shadows steps a tall stooped figure who says, "Hi boys, I'm Osama and I'd like to stand." Imagine too if he was successful. No, the vital need for democracy doesn't wash either.

With their credibility being exposed by these possible untruths, the leaders changed thrust again, stressing now how important it had been to effect a 'regime change' for the good of the local people, the region and world. Nodding agreement with a sage wisdom that was obviously beyond them, the still-compliant souls never dared question and raise the fact that there seemed to be some inconsistencies here. When Sadaam had been gassing the Kurds, nothing was done, he was an ally then. When millions were being slaughtered in Ruanda, nothing ... the cruelty of Bokassa in Central Africa Republic, nothing, Mugabe in Zimbabwe, nothing, the tragedies of Darfur, nothing. At times, these same leaders would say that the sovereignty of other nations is sacrosanct and not something they have a mandate to interfere with. The memory of the masses is so short and selective. The repressive regimes of Papa Doc and Baby Doc in Haiti were tolerated, yet Grenada was invaded because the opposition politicians asked them to do so. Figure that one!!!!

With thoughts and questions like these, Phaedrus would have moved up the Top 50 list and no doubt would have made Number One. You can see that the perception of right depends on what you are being told. For us, it was sad. We didn't believe in the legality or right of the war in Iraq but admired the valour and sacrifice being made by the American people. It was because of that sacrifice that we didn't comment or try to 'make our point'. I believed that each man and woman we met, was right in their heart and should be respected and admired for that. I just hoped I didn't get on a list of 50 for having such thoughts.

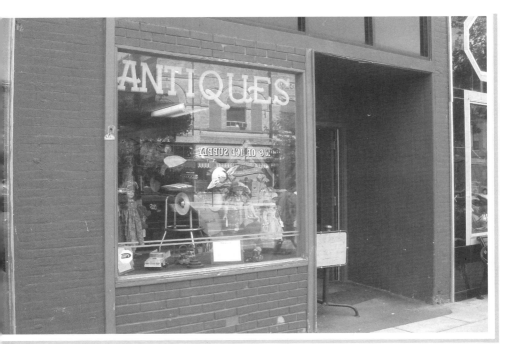

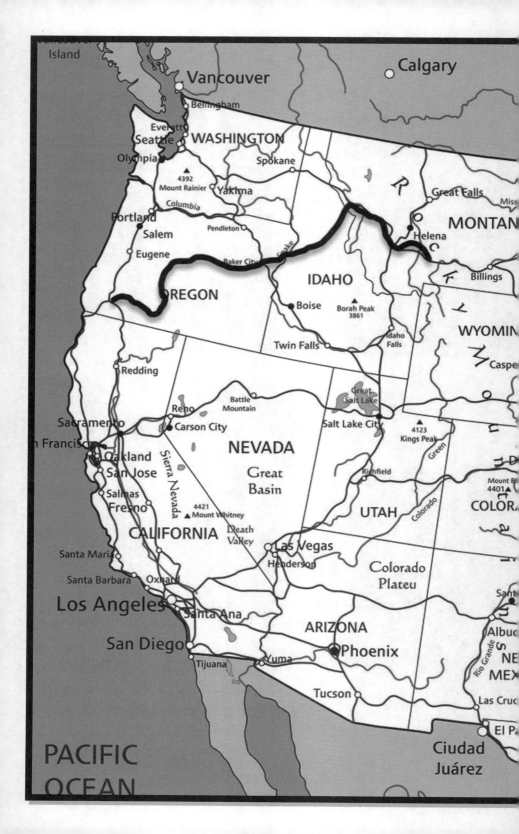

Chapter Nine

ACROSS TO OREGON

W e'd decided on an early start with a breakfast on the way somewhere. We headed north with Pirsig struggling with his thoughts and relating how his discovery of Jules Henri Poincare came about. He'd intensely studied the history of philosophy for more than a year before finding Poincare and the discovery that there is continuity between their thoughts and beliefs. Poincare's path of discovery stops exactly where Pirsig's starts. He was thrilled, like "Robinson Crusoe's discovery of footprints on the sand." We were heading a little north, and it wasn't very warm, but we stuck to it. A job's a job, after all. We paused

briefly to look at a real log cabin, an old settler's one with grass growing on the roof. The logs were all very irregular in size and shape so the walls were not straight. It had dirt floors and mud caulking between the logs. This was the sort of place that would have been the normal shelter for the travellers in the area a couple of hundred years ago. As with the halved-Chautauqua, we passed by the Lewis and Clark caverns in a narrow canyon past Three Forks, then slogged up a long grade and over the Continental Divide. This is the spine of the US, also known as the Great Divide. The rivers on the eastern side, the ones we'd been following, flow all the way back to the Atlantic Ocean or the Gulf of Mexico. Over the top, and the rivers will take you to the Pacific. Lewis and Clark were trying to find a way through that wouldn't be too hard, and if there was a place where the sources of two big rivers weren't too far apart, how good would that be? As it happens the Columbia/Snake does go 1,250 miles out to the Pacific and the Yellowstone/Missouri/Mississippi goes from not far away, and finally exits in the Gulf of Mexico more than 2,500 miles away. We didn't pause, it was cold and we were on a roll. About an hour and a half was enough for the first session of the day. It had brought us to Butte, another of the big towns of Montana, another real city, its past glories based on copper and a couple of legendary brothels. We found a place for pancakes, amazed that it was nearly full on a Thursday morning.

Squeezing in next to a group of old duffers, we were soon warmer and happier. Kitty filmed a family group, including kids in cowboy hats, which seemed odd to us of course, but quite normal for them. A garrulous old-timer from beside us wanted to know what we were doing, where we were from etc. He mets with his buddies every day for breakfast and usually another meal as well. His name was Joe and he wants to talk, OK by us. He told us that Myles and I would be good workers because we ate our food fast, he had observed. He told us that this is how the Russians hire their workers. Later, he even followed us out to the bikes … still talking. He had taken a bit of a shine to Myles, and they end up swapping some money. I recorded him as Mouthy Joe in meagre notes of the day, a nomenclature Myles had bestowed on him. As always, a stack of pancakes each went down a treat. There may be no goodness in them, but as a foundation for further riding on a cool day, there was real goodness. They fuelled the machine, so to speak.

Later we paused at a resort called Fairmont, and Kitty and I had a swim in the hot pools. It was largely deserted this day, so my exposed hirsute torso only frightened a smallish number of people, hopefully not scarring them for life. At moments like this, I often think of an English journalist (whose name I have forgotten) who'd had occasion to be shirtless in China and an old woman couldn't resist stroking his hairy arm, giggling and jabbering away such that all her peers were also laughing good-naturedly. When he asked what had been said, he was told that she'd exclaimed that she didn't know that gorillas spoke English. It was great to glide along in a big swimming pool that could have accommodated hundreds, glasses off, seeing nothing but a few blurred figures off in the distance. There was also an outdoor area with a water-slide, but I preferred just to lounge in the hot, hot water.

When fully pinked, we moved on again following the scenic Montana State Route 1. It is a small road for tourists, taking in notable backwater places, the first and most significant being Anaconda where we had lunch. Whist we experienced the same entry to the town as the others, by passing down the valley past the great brick smoke stack of the old copper smelter, our repast in no way compared with their good restaurant steak and coffee. The radially-bricked stack still towers 600 ft over the town. It was the tallest brick structure of any kind in the world when built in 1919 and is still thought to be the tallest free-standing brick structure. This was the home of the Anaconda Copper Mining Company which, in the 1920s was the fourth-largest corporation in the world. The town has a population of about 9,000, and proclaims that its main street meets the mountains. I'd have thought that, with an elevation of more than 5,300 ft it was in the mountains. It certainly felt that way, as we struggled in with cold rain hurrying us along. The urgency to find somewhere to eat and shelter may have influenced the decision to stop at Joe's. It was there, it was convenient, it was empty … and it was awful. My dear old Mum always said, "If you can't say something nice about someone, don't say anything." Sorry, Mum, but there is also 'name them and shame them'. The attendant may or may not have been Joe. He was pleasant and we would have loved to have liked his meals, but these were right up there with Jeremy's in Canada. There was nothing redeemable about our stop here other than that we were inside. Of course, Myles and Kitty both proclaimed that I had ignored what looked like a much better place. Sorry team, I was a bit tunnel-visioned. I'd seen shelter, the mind computed … need shelter, need shelter now – so Joe's it was to our regret. I often reflect on these absolutely horrible dining experiences and wonder how they can get it so wrong. I am an easy person to please. Our little town of a few hundred in Golden Bay has several flourishing cafés offering good fare to travellers. They have variety and if you did want a pie and chips, you could still find that ... but most palettes are more sophisticated these days and you're more likely to find chicken, apricot and brie paninis being bought. You could have crusty rolls, croissants, spinach and almond quiches, feta and walnut pinwheels, all sorts of filo parcels, spanakopita, roti, somosas, wraps and baps. What you couldn't get is the abysmal fare that Joe's and Jeremy's served up.

We struggled along for another hour and a bit, in mildly unpleasant going. Geographically, it was fine, always something to look at, trees, mountains and lakes, but meteorologically it was crappy, cold, wet and sometimes windy. The sun did come out wanly and we possibly had a better time of it than our predecessors, when we reach Hall, which is little more than a dot on the map. They'd been tired too, wanting a rest, and they sheltered out of the wind on the lee side of the church, spreading out their jackets to lie on. Chris turned his face to his jacket to sleep.

Pirsig finds it lonely without the Sutherlands and runs away with Poincare, Kant, Euclid and Reiman in his mind, wanting to talk Chautauqua until the loneliness passes. He gets pretty deep with geometric axioms and whether they are experimental verities or not. It is seven pages before they're back on their bike and heading for Missoula. There is some good stuff in there, but do you need to want to know about the struggle of Poincare and Phaedrus as they worked on their respective puzzles of interpreting the harmony of the cosmos. Our break was only interesting for the reason that they also stopped there. There was nothing to see, nowhere to walk and the church was locked.

We rode on to Missoula, where Chris had spotted the large M on the hill. It was still there, high above the university campus. Missoula is the second city of Montana and accordingly big with a population close to 100,000, which means it had all the attendant problems of traffic and navigation ... making it not enjoyable for us. We were just passing through but needed supplies for the night. We were undecided as to whether or not we should try to camp out on the logging road that they did in 1968. We were cold and not as buoyed with success as we usually were. Our navigation was a bit hit and miss, and it is a struggled finding the way out of town and a supermarket. Ultimately both were done. I found some local beer called Moose Drool and got a six pack to give Myles a change. He is a Heineken man, and it was hard to get him to accept change. I think he was a little wary in case he found a substitute that was nicer, leading to supply problems. We'd turned to the south west and would be entering the Bitterroot National Forest – this was The Rockies. The landscape was now fir trees and rocky outcrops, bluffs and hills and mountains layered away into the distance almost wherever we looked. Late afternoon, we reached Lolo Pass. This is where they interacted with another touring couple on a bike. It was the sort of fleeting contact that happens all the time with motorcyclists, but I like the way Pirsig records it.

> At Lolo Pass we see a restaurant, and pull up in front of it beside an old Harley high-miler. It has a homemade pannier on the back and thirty six thousand on the odometer. A real cross-country man.
>
> Inside we fill up on pizza and milk and when finished leave right away. There's not much sunlight left, and a search for a campsite after dark is difficult and unpleasant.
>
> As we leave we see the cross-country man by the cycles with his wife and we say hello. He is from Missouri, and the relaxed look on his wife's face tells me they've been having a good trip.
>
> The man asks, "Were you bucking that wind up to Missoula too?"
>
> I nod. "It must have been thirty or forty miles an hour."
>
> "At least," he says.

We talk about camping for a while and they comment on how cold it is. They never dreamed in Missouri it would be this cold in the summer, even in the mountains. They've had to buy clothes and blankets.

"It shouldn't be too cold tonight," I say. "We're only at about five thousand feet."

Chris says, "We're going to camp just down the road."

"At one of the campsites?"

"No, just somewhere off the road," I say.

They show no inclination of wanting to join us, so after a pause I press the starter button and we wave off.

For us, we were just a little dispirited by the cold, and decided that when we see the Lolo Hot Springs sign with a campsite opposite, nothing could be finer than a nice little cabin and another soak in a thermal pool. Ironically, neither happen,ed as the cabins were all full and by the time we got the tents up the spa was closed and we'de lost a little of the impetus anyway. Kitty climbed a bluff and meditated for a while, high above us, later admitting to being a little worried about the coyotes and also about finding her way back down to us. We met our own high-milers here. Lyall on an old BMW 90/6 from the 70s and Trooper were from Red Lodge and were escaping for a week or so from family and work. Lyall had already seen our bikes in Red Lodge, noticing them because he is a Beemer man. They seemed pleased to find them here. We bonded immediately. This happens on occasion … when you enjoy a short meeting of minds or a shared experience. I suppose it is a watered-down group 'love at first sight'. We liked these fellow travellers and shared tales and anecdotes, a little like a Chautauqua. They were young guys (In Myles's and my eyes, quite old in Kitty's eyes) who worked hard in the snow/tourist arena that is Red Lodge for the winter. Each year in the summer, they rewarded themselves with a small adventure away on the bikes. We shared the trivia that make each day, just like Pirsig and his high-miler did. Lyall had had to get a new

ZEN AND THE LAST HURRAH

tyre for the back of the Beemer, which he managed that day in Missoula. We shared, too, the fire they'd lit to cook their food on. There was a lot of mirth because they didn't really know what they were doing, but fire and food go well together.

Another BMW owner from Montana was in the camp, but not on his bike, so although he joined the group, it was almost like he was an outsider – because he was talking the talk, not walking the walk. He was a little too much of a try-hard to enamour himself completely to us. Probably a nice guy, but overcompensating for not being aboard two wheels. Watching the flickering flames, we moaned about the poor standard of dining we'd encountered so far, and the boys enjoyed that. "It's nine to one!" they chorused. They had analysed this from their previous trips and reckon that just randomly stopping and dining on the road without recourse to prior knowledge or guidance from others results in nine poor meals for each good one. We reckoned they were about right and gently asserted that in New Zealand we reckoned those same figures are juxtaposed. The night was cold, so we all moved close to the fire, easy and companionable. We yarned. It would be a cosy memory for all of us, although Myles didn't like the Moose Drool.

What wasn't cosy was the night. It was bitter, and the frost in the morning confirmed it. Tenting is not always pleasant. It can be cold like this night, it is often a little uncomfortable and usually cramped when there are two of you in a two-man tent. Kitty was still complaining about sharing with the "hairy, snoring mammoth". She had not yet decided on which end was worse to be near. She had tried topping and tailing … and she had tried heads together – but didn't like the rumbling nocturnal emissions from either end. Myles had graciously offered to share his tent with me, leaving her to enjoy splendid solitude, but the thought of our hirsute bodies touching in the night and sticking like Velcro was all too much for me. The status quo would remain. We were shaded under the high bluff Kitty climbed, but the hot pools complex across the road was bathed in early morning sunshine when we woke. We enjoyed the half mile walk across to it in search of the now regulation pancake stack. This straightened out the creaky bits and warmed us slightly. The dining area was big and dark and the wooden walls lined with photos from earlier times. They were interesting enough and gave a feel for the area and the harder times past. A couple arrived on their Harley. It had been an early start for them from Missoula, and now they wanted warming and breakfast.

"Pretty cold out there," I led with.

"Hell yes," said the (presumed) wife, "I've had to turn on my electric vest!"

Shared sympathy lowered a little with this, but it was the way with the more modern touring bikes. The rider probably had heated hand grips as well and could even have had an electrically heated seat. We felt like positive Luddites on our bare-bones machines, my bike not even having electric start. The engine's cylinders do stick out in the wind just in front of my feet though, so there are never cold feet for BMW riders. We had no wind shields and would suffer the piercing cold for a while today until the sun's rays warmed the air. But with regular stops, we would manage. We always have in the past, we would do so today.

We might have had a cold night, but Pirsig had a disturbed night with a recurring dream. It was his 'glass door' dream where he is in a funeral sarcophagus with his family on the other side of a glass door. He was pleased to be awake and when he finally rolled Chris over, he told him it was a great day but to dress with everything on as it would be a chilly ride. He also tells us it will be a long Chautauqua today, one that he has been looking forward to during the whole trip. The way he slips in and out of reality is sometimes easy, sometimes hard. It is like a playground with some apparatus just for the little kids but with some available for super-athletes to do gymnastic activities on the parallel bars and high rings like the competitors in the Olympic Games. Both little ones and experts enjoy the same place with equal enjoyment. ZAMM allows me to challenge myself and be stretched … but still pull back when it gets too hard. Today, he leads off with some good easy thoughts.

Second gear and then third. Not too fast on these curves. Beautiful sunlight on these forests.

There has been a haze, a backup problem in this Chautauquq so far; I talked about caring the first day and then realised I couldn't say anything meaningful about caring until its inverse side, Quality, is understood. I think it's important now to tie care to Quality by pointing out that care and Quality are internal and external aspects of the same thing. A person who sees Quality and feels it as he works is a person who cares. A person who cares about what he sees and does is a person who is bound to have some characteristics of Quality.

One last thing amused us from this night camp. Next to us had been a big fifth-wheeler with an older, big, tough-looking guy who had looked so out of place walking a tiny lap-dog. We thought there was a wife, but we never saw evidence of her. Myles yarned with him in the morning sun. This was an old Harley rider, as prejudiced as it ever gets. He told Myles that the riders of the 'Jap stuff' … and in fact anything that wasn't a Harley, were "panty waste … milk bread". Not a lot we could say about that. We laughed and left.

The road led through the low-level Lolo Pass itself, and we put an chilly hour or so under our belt before pausing. We were cold again, but the day promised so much. We were now in Idaho. The isolation that riding brings often means that little bits of silliness rise to the surface. Today, I didn't seem to have a song to sing, but I kept calling out "Idahoooo" repetitively at the top of my voice as we swept along. At our first stop, we jointly laughed at the seemingly puerile slogan on the local number plates. Idaho – Famous Potatoes. All the other states have heralded their most famous scenic beauty or similar, and Idaho just wanted to announce that all they're good for is … potatoes. We've had *Michigan – Great Lakes State, Wisconsin – America's Dairyland, Minnesota – 10,000 Lakes, North Dakota – Peace Garden State, South Dakota – Great Faces, Great Places, Wyoming – Like No Place on Earth, Montana – Big Sky Country,* all of which are evocative of something to be proud of. I'm probably selling the spud farmers a little short here, but supplying McD's with umpteen trillion fries doesn't really rate like telling everyone that you have 10,000 lakes in your state, does it? Of course, before we'd be done, we'd also pass through *The Pacific Wonderland* and *The Golden State.*

That human need to sloganise our states, cities, towns, villages etc. brings back fond memories of earlier travels. In 1977 in Mexico's Palenque region on the Yucatan Peninsula, we had met and enjoyed an American named Tom Beers. We may have only known him for two or three days, but he remains vivid in my memory. Steph and I, with my brother Roly and friend Lawrie, were camping out in the carpark beside a pretty waterfall that had a swimming pool in front of it and a Tarzan cave behind. We were resting and happy to have someone new in our lives. Tom had suffered scarlet fever as a youth, leaving him with no body hairs – none on his head, no chest hairs, no eyebrows, nothing. That made him slightly unusual, but not overly so. Tom was the first Vietnam War veteran we'd ever come across face to face to talk to. He told us of his experiences, the fears and what it was like being a conscript in a far-away war that he and very few of his peers believed in. We learned how they would stay in camp as much as possible, very reluctant to venture out into the jungles … and when they did, they'd make as much noise as they could so as not to surprise anyone. They felt no one wanted them to be there, and every Vietnamese person was seen as a potential enemy. Tom said most of his unit spent their time trying to get through their tour by being stoned as much as possible. Marijuana use was not just rife, it was the normal way, something we'd heard before but not from the horse's mouth. Tom was from a small, sloganised, hick town somewhere, and he told us it was his mission to have it changed. The town proclaimed itself to be The Home of *Fred MacMurray*. He was that cheesy actor who featured in numerous low-grade films and TV shows, including the inane *My Three Sons*. That whole genre of puke-inducing entertainment was hugely popular with mainstream simpletons and spinster aunts. Tom wanted to really put his town on the map with it to be known in the future as *The Home of Tom Beers – The Man Who Shot Fred MacMurray*. It could have been the magic mushrooms he fed us, but at the time we found it hilarious. We hadn't come across Americans who were happy to laugh at themselves before.

We followed a winding river on a road that was almost deserted. As we warmed, our enjoyment grew. It was a gentle sweeping and swaying sort of morning. We were not scratching, we were just cruising, easily banking into the bends, leaning in and lifting out, enjoying the experience and looking around. The view was close, not away in the distance as we'd had before. This was the Bitterroot Mountains, leading to the Nez Perce Forest. We'd not heard the name Nez Perce before last night, when the boys told us of the Indian tribe of that name and how they'd been the largest tribe in the area who had many permanent villages even though they were migratory. They became part of US history that reflects poorly on the white man. The non-aggressive Nez Perce fought strategic battles as they retreated up into Canada. 13 battles were fought before they surrendered at Chinook after what was the last fight between the Indian nations and the US Government. Their flight path is now known as the Nez Perce National Historic Trail, and there is a commemorative ride in the Cypress Hills each June. There was a commemorative monument up ahead. Myles alerted us to a snake that was on the road, the first we've seen. We passed a sign that told us the road ahead was winding for 72 miles. Wow! The day warmed and we brewed up by the river. This river we'd been following is a tributary of Snake River which leads into the Columbia and flows all the way out through Portland to the Pacific. Meanwhile, we just kept purring through canyons and slowly losing altitude. We were coming off the high inland plains. It was not too cold, not too hot ... as Goldilocks would have said, "It was just right". Myles declared it the best road he'd ever ridden. I hesitate to agree, possibly wanting to appear more worldly. I have ridden fabulous roads around the world and can clearly recall a wonderful day in Mexico that, at the time, I felt would never be matched. Thoughts flick to other wonderful rides in the Pyrenees, the Andes, Northern Pakistan, Greece, New Zealand's South Island, Norway ... yet I can't counter with a decidedly superior choice. It was that good. I think he's right – it would be hard to get more pleasure from two wheels.

Young Chris wanted to write a letter home to Mom, and when initially

he didn't know what to write, Pirsig told him to make a list of what he'd like to tell her about, then later they could put the list in order of importance and develop the important ones. Chris went from not knowing what to write to making a list three pages long of the things he wanted to write about. This reminded Pirsig of his earlier experiences with a dull student back in his Bozeman teaching days when she couldn't write one page about the US, yet once directed to write a page about the front wall of a local store, the mental block was broken. Later, Pirsig had his students writing whole essays about the face on a coin. This problem of getting stuck by the anticipation of the task set him off onto quite an interesting diatribe.

Stuckness. That's what I want to talk about today.

Back on our trip out of Miles City you'll remember I talked about how formal scientific method could be applied to the repair of a motorcycle through the study of chains of cause and effect and the application of experimental method to determine these chains The purpose then was to show what was meant by classic rationality.

Now I want to show that that classic pattern of rationality can be tremendously improved, expanded and made far more effective through the formal recognition of Quality in its operation. Before doing this, however, I should go over some of the negative aspects of traditional maintenance to show just where the problems are.

The first is stuckness, a mental stuckness that accompanies the physical stuckness of whatever it is you're working on. The same thing Chris was suffering from. A screw sticks, for example on a side cover assembly. You check the manual to see if there might be any special cause for this screw to come off so hard, but all it says is " Remove side cover plate" in that wonderful terse technical style that never tells you what you want to know. There's no earlier procedure left undone that might cause the cover screws to stick.

If you're experienced you'd probably apply a penetrating liquid and an impact at this point. But suppose you're inexperienced and you attach a self-locking plier wrench to the shank of your screwdriver and really twist it hard, a procedure you've had success with in the past, but which this time succeeds only in tearing the slot in the screw.

Your mind was already thinking ahead to what you would do when the cover plate was off, and so it takes a little time to realise that this irritating minor annoyance of a torn screw slot isn't just irritating and minor. You're stuck. Stopped. Terminated. It's absolutely stopped you from fixing the motorcycle.

This isn't a rare scene in science or technology. This is the commonest scene of all. Just plain stuck. In traditional maintenance this is the worst of all moments, so bad that you have avoided even thinking about it before you come to it.

The book is no good to you now. Neither is scientific reason. You don't need any scientific experiments to find out what's wrong. It's obvious what's wrong. What you need is an hypothesis for how you're going to get that slotless screw out of there and scientific reason method doesn't provide any of these hypotheses. It operates only after they're around.

This is the zero moment of consciousness. Stuck. No answer. Honked. Kaput. It's a miserable experience emotionally. You're losing time. You're incompetent. You don't know what you're doing. You should be ashamed of yourself. You should take the machine to a real mechanic who knows how to figure these things out.

It's normal at this point for the fear-anger syndrome to take over and make you want to hammer on that side-plate with a chisel, to pound it off with a sledge if necessary. You think about it, and the more you think about it the more you're inclined to take the whole machine to a high bridge and drop it off. It's just outrageous that a tiny slot of a screw can defeat you so totally.

What you're up against is the great unknown, the void of all Western thought. You need some ideas, some hypotheses. Traditional scientific method, unfortunately, has never quite gotten around to saying exactly where to pick up more of these hypotheses. Traditional scientific method has always been at the very best, 20-20 hindsight. It is good for seeing where you've been. It's good for testing the truth of what you think you know, but it can't tell you where you ought to go, unless where you ought to go is a continuation of where you were going in the past. Creativity, originality, inventiveness, intuition, imagination –"unstuckness." in other words – are completely outside its domain.

I often think about what he says, sometimes nodding agreement and understanding, but what I can't do is think like him. There'll be no 'deep and meaningfuls' come from this trip from me. No new revelations or theories for mankind to debate. On the simple stuff, I sometimes modify his thoughts where they clash with mine. The night before, young Chris had asked his dad what he should be when he grows up and Pirsig answered "Honest". I've always wished 'happiness' to be the state my children would grow to. I spent a little time thinking whether I'd be OK with any of the kids being 'happy and dishonest'. I reasoned it could happen, so had to modify my wishes to a half-Pirsig – 'happy and honest'.

This was a great day to be riding, it was stimulating and enjoyable, yet mellow in that it wasn't challenging or demanding. It was so easy and cruisy that I was happy enough to forgive Pirsig the eight pages of analysis and doctrine before he actually solves, the 'unstuckness' of the screw.

What your actual solution is is unimportant as long as it has Quality. Thoughts about the screw as combined rigidness and adhesiveness and its special helical interlock might lead naturally to impaction and the use of solvents. That is one kind of Quality track. Another track may be to go to the library and look through a catalogue of mechanic's tools in which you might come across a screw extractor that might do the job. Or to call a friend who knows something about mechanical work. Or just to drill the screw out, or just burn it out with a torch. Or you might just, as a result of your meditative attention to the screw, come up with some new way of extracting it that has never been thought of before and that beats all the rest and is patentable and makes you a millionaire five years from now. There's no predicting what's on that Quality track. The solutions are all simple - after you have arrived at them. But they're simple only when you know already what they are.'

He's long-winded but quite perceptive. Meanwhile, we forked off Highway 12 onto Highway 13 gently climbing again up a wide valley and in the early afternoon, rolled into Grangeville. Kitty had unexpectedly got a case of diarrhoea, and luckily we were able to stop at a supermarket, fortunately with suitably close and easily accessed toilets. Young Chris had also suffered similarly but a day earlier and with worse results. We admired Kitty for sticking to the storyline. While in the carpark after reprovisioning, we met and talked with an elderly lady with an enormous 1965 Oldsmobile Eighty Eight convertible. We commented on how unusual it was to have three 1965 vehicles together out doing daily business. We were not on a 'vintage' run, we were going cross-country on a mission and, hey, it was a nice day, so she'd gone shopping … with the hood down. It was an enormous barge of a thing that would need this type of parking area … or you just wouldn't park. To parallel park it at the sidewalk would be a nightmare. You could imagine folk going off to work in the morning in one and returning at morning tea time because they hadn't been able to find a park. There would be a lot of streets back home where she couldn't drive this leviathan. Grangeville rates a mention in ZAMM because it is where Pirsig noticed a stunningly gorgeous high-schooler in a restaurant, making eyes at a young male, while another girl behind the counter glares, thinking that no-one is seeing her anger. A triangle, he mused … thinking how they kept passing unseen through little moments of other people's lives.

The afternoon's ride was different, as after a while out in the hot afternoon sun climbing again, the prairie broke into a canyon, just as described in ZAMM, and a then huge descent followed down past several prominently signposted truck run-offs, each spaced a few miles apart. The run-offs looked so inviting as they were steep, uphill dead-ends leading into soft sand traps with a presumably redundant big concrete barrier above that. There would be a massive bottoming as you'd begin the steep uphill slow-down, big G forces, then the spectacular dust show as you'd hit the sand trap. They could easily sell tickets, you can imagine the barker: "Roll up, roll up. Ride the big rig on a death-defying drop! See how far you can go!" All of them were immaculately groomed with not even footprints in the sand. This downhill was almost physically breathtaking. There were maybe a hundred or more switchback turns and as Pirsig noted, we must have dropped several thousand feet. It was unlike any other downhill I have done. The views were stunning and wide to a horizon. A short but pleasant afternoon stop was had in the tiny old-West town of Riggins. It was now a white-water rafting place of note but still only had a few hundred residents. Ice creams were devoured, the first of the trip that I could remember, they were so welcome. Not far out of town had been an intriguing sign, 'Yahweh 666 Warning Assembly'. Much later, I reference the sole-practitioner's website. At a quick glance it looked like being harder to follow than even ZAMM. He is a loony who camps out in the hills, proclaiming that Jesus is the Son of Satan. As they often say, "Only in America, folks!"

It was a long day that was by no means over. The road climbed again, this time into pine forests. Late in the afternoon we paused in Cambridge and get a few more supplies. The night's stay was in a camp about 20 miles away on the road across towards Oregon. Brownlee Campground is a very basic facility close into the hills. Here, young Chris Pirsig was put to bed on a picnic table. This seemed odd until we arrived, and the tables were noticed as being really quite large. One thing we found a little strange was that, in 1968, they rode out from Cambridge after having supper and had to ride the last part after dark. It was a long way to go in the dark if you are just looking for somewhere to sleep, as they were. Perhaps Pirsig already knew of the Brownlee Campground. This had been a long day, but a great day. I noted in my Palm One PDA, "best day yet".

The next morning was cool but nice, just like in 1968. We liked these sorts of crude camps that the State Parks offer, with the most basic of facilities – usually just a source of water and a couple of toilets. This one was a half mile or so off the road up a gravel track. No shop, no ranger, a creek to wash in, each camping area big enough for two or three tents and separated from others by trees and thick scrub. There were a couple of other cars tucked away in the dense greenery, snug and private. It was here that Pirsig let Chris sleep until the sun reached him and then hollered, "WAKE!", following that up with a recital from the *Rubaiyat of Omar Khayyam* ... to the confusion of the freshly awakened 12-year-old. Today, Kitty filmed birds and the stream, while we cooked breakfast. As well as our Thermette which we used purely for boiling water, we had an Optimus 8R Hunter, beloved of motorcyclists and hikers for generations. I have used them for many years because of the tidy way they fold to a square, easily packed shape, and most of all because of their ability to run on the petrol from the bike's tank. As they heat, the tank pressurises and the burning gets fiercer and fiercer, roaring with a blue flame. They're fondly known as 'the old chuffer' by some because of that roaring. This one I'd had for quite a few years and it had done sterling service on this trip. A fellow camper told us that a bear has been sighted just along the track. Something to tell the folks at home, we thought and left shortly afterwards, still thinking of whether to run with the pack on or not. "To jettison, or not to jettison? That is the question. Whether 'tis nobler to suffer the claws and teeth of an outraged bear, pack on back ... or throw and run?"

We pressed on into Oregon along Highway 96. Another bewilderingly, interesting and varied day followed with the highlight being riding across to and down through Hells Canyon. It wasn't as long as yesterday's descent but it iwas spectacular and like a mystery – unfolding as you weren't quite sure which part of the stunning landscape you were heading into next. We twisted and turned and dropped to the river, which we had seen from on-high earlier. It was hot and the countryside tan and rocky with small stunted dark-green trees. Afterwards, we stopped for petrol and a respite from the excitement. We've never claimed to be mature … and we took photos of a shop's sign that says Crappie Stop. This must have a different meaning to folk out here. It gently amused our puerile minds. To Pirsig, the arid semi-desert country here reminded him of Rajasthan in Northern India. I haven't been to Rajasthan, but it is a little like parts of Northern Pakistan that I travelled across on *The Last Hurrah* ride in 2005. It was here in the semi-desert sitting on what he described as an Omar Khayyam rock, waiting for Chris to come back from a diarrhoea dash into the bushes, that Pirsig reflected that he felt not bad. I think that is as contented as he gets, which I feel a little sad about.

> *Let's get off Omar and onto the Chautauqua. Omar's solution is just to sit around and guzzle the wine and feel so bad that time is passing and the Chautauqua looks good to me by comparison. Particularly today's Chautauqua, which is about gumption.*

Most people thought that we were just sitting on our bums and riding across the US, drinking beer and having fun. Well yes, there was that, but with ZAMM never far from my hands, it was often like being in a congregation before an inspirational preacher. We'd learned about classic and romantic understanding, we were awash with Quality with a capital Q, we learned about the Church of Reason, we'd been treated to being 'stuck' and the solution to it. We were still learning and not yet aware how it would all be tied together and ultimately packaged. Pirsig was still drip-feeding us the road-trip tale, he was drip-feeding us a hell of a lot more though. I'd been impatient to date, but now needed to slow down, we'd only got five days to go to get to San Francisco. It was now important to savour every morsel. He'd still got a lot to say.

I like the word "gumption" because it's so homely and so forlorn and so out of style it looks as if it needs a friend and isn't likely to reject anyone who comes along. It's an old Scottish word, once used a lot by pioneers, but which, like "kin" seems to have all but dropped out of use. I like it also because it describes exactly what happens to someone who connects with Quality. He gets filled with gumption.

The Greeks called it enthousiasmos, the root of "enthusiasm," which means literally "filled with theos," or God, or Quality. See how that fits?

A person filled with gumption doesn't sit around dissipating and stewing about things. He's at the front of the train of his own awareness, watching to see what's up the track and meeting it when it comes. That's gumption.

I like it when later Pirsig calls gumption, "psychic gasoline" and an absolute necessity when it comes to mending a motorcycle. He also contemplates the idea of starting a whole new academic field called gumptionology where he would sort the gumption traps, categorise and structure them into hierarchies for the edification of future generations. He'd like to see in a college catalogue: 'Gumptionology 101 – an examination of affective, cognitive and psychomotor blocks in the perception of Quality relationships – 3 cr, VII, MWF.' I like his gumption stuff being as it is something I relate to and the examples he works with are real and relevant to me. I smile though at his fairly anal way of describing meticulously the way to not fall into the gumption trap of out-of-sequence-reassembly setback. Telling us that it is a good idea to always have a notebook on hand while you are taking things apart ... noting the order they are in, the colours of the wires etc. doesn't take him long for a change, only half a page or so. His other technique for avoiding the out-of-sequence-reassembly gumption trap is actually quite good and smart but simple. He recommends laying out on the workshop floor or bench newspaper and the parts, as they as disassembled, are laid out in the direction we read, going across to the right and down in lines. To reassemble, you work the opposite way. Not bad, better than throwing the bits in little tubs or boxes confident that you'll remember the order when the time comes. His listed setbacks of out-of-sequence reassembly, intermittent failure and parts problems are only the 'external' cause of gumption loss. Once he gets onto the 'internal' gumption traps of 'truth traps' and 'muscle traps', Pirsig really starts to get the bit between his teeth and expound all sorts of wisdom.

Neither of us stopped at Baker City, we'd got a big day to complete. A snack was later had at the tiny, almost deserted settlement of Unity, a short five or six mile ride off from the highway. Pirsig also fuelled up here mentioning only the hot black road and the sage-bush. For us in 2006, it was notable for the meagre pickings food-wise, chewing the fat with some other motorcyclists also in for petrol, and for the 'no dog pooing' sign on the front window. Why they needed a sign in a place that can't

have more than a handful of people through in a day escaped us. Or do they think that without the sign, folk would fetch up from all over with dogs galore to deposit faeces on the forecourt?

Prairie City was hot and just as Pirsig described it. They'd stopped and Chris had worked on his letter, using the list prepared earlier. We just noted the wide main street and view to the town's namesake and move on. Dayville was passed through before another forgettable meal in the late afternoon at Mitchell, a small village remembered because of the encounter with Henry, the huge brown bear who was caged opposite the diner. He belonged to the diner as some sort of promotional, neon-sign replacement, I think. Standing tall, he easily towered over us, maybe half as tall again. We all felt a bit sorry for Henry, thinking he would be better off back in Yellowstone Park collecting backpacks. Resting in the cooling, almost twilight, we talked with a despondent cyclist who had been struggling in the heat, probably suffering 'the second day slump' that Pirsig warned the Sutherlands of before they started out.

There was still another 75 miles to Bend, where we were going to call it quits, so we couldn't dally. The others had pushed on another 25 miles past Bend, but we knew we would be almost fully-shot by then, and now neither bike had a fully-functioning headlight. It was times like this that you'd rather just stop. Knowing this would then give us too much of a handicap the next day, we don't. Instead we pushed ourselves to finish the day. It wasn't great ... I don't think anyone enjoyed it. We reached Bend as it darkened completely and we got lost, got grumpy and found places that were full or not suited. After an age and a mini-saga involving hiding in a vacant lot, walking the streets, riding without lights in the quite large metropolis of 75,000 people ... we negotiated with a woman from the Asian subcontinent to stay in her brother's motel ... just down the road. In New Zealand we have a series of popular beer advertising billboards that always end with ... yeah right! They are always a cynical rebuttal of

ACROSS TO OREGON
219

the lead phrase. In a prominent university town, one was "Lots of people take six years to graduate ... yeah right!" Here, we could have applied "Just down the road ... yeah right!" Ultimately, though, we were ensconced in a mid-priced motel unit without having any encounters with officers of the law. It was a relief and spirits soon rise. So much so, that we all rang home to New Zealand late in the evening. It had been a good if hard 300 miles.

Sunday morning 21 August brought the realisation that, in a week's time, Myles and I would be heading for the airport. In the meantime, there was still a bit of both the ride, and ZAMM to go. It was chilly when we first headed away and not really pleasant, but the day promised to warm up and be a scorcher. We'd decided to put in a biggish first spell to Diamond Lake before our main breakfast of pancakes. We learned at our first fill-up of the day that Oregon law meant that there must be a pump attendant do the petrol pumping. It seemed to be a combination of safety issues, with the threat of litigation being lessened when there were trained personnel involved, and it was also an employment initiative to provide more work. Most motorcyclists don't find it acceptable to have any old pump jockey spilling petrol on their fancy paint jobs and most pump guys similarly don't want the responsibility of filling a customised chopper tank that might have cost a couple of thousand dollars. This has led to a charade where the attendant attends but wants you to do the pumping but it has to be discreetly managed because they also don't want other motorists to spot that they aren't complying with state law. This was the only state where we had encountered this requirement.

It was a straight and not very interesting ride through forested countryside. Maybe if we'd been warm, we'd have been singing and loving it. What we did love, however, was Diamond Lake when we got to it. It was just picture postcard perfect, smooth and like a mirror, reflecting Mount Bailey behind. There was still a bit of snow on the hills and with the vivid blue of the sky above it was exquisite. We parked and walked across

the waterfront sands to the dining hall of a resort hotel. Kitty filmed a humming bird. This wasn't the lake that our antecedents argued at. They'd gone to Crater Lake just a few miles away. The days were now getting Chris down, and he was asking why they were doing this, just riding and riding. His father had said it was to see the country … to vacation. But they both know that wasn't true. We'd already noticed the riding seemed to have an intensity to it that was growing. Pirsig had had a nightmare last night which frightened Chris and he recalled it.

> We're outside. There's a motorcycle here. I think we're in Oregon somewhere.
> "I'm all right, it was just a nightmare."
> He continues to cry and I sit quietly with him for a while. "It's all right," I say, but he doesn't stop. He's badly frightened.
> So am I.
> "What were you dreaming about?"
> "Who was it?"
> "I'm not sure."
> Chris's crying stops, but he continues to shake from the cold. "Did you see his face?"
> "It was my own face, Chris, that's when I shouted … It was just a bad dream." I tell him he is shivering and should get back into the sleeping bag. He does this. "It's so cold," he says.

"Yes." By the dawn light I can see the vapor from our breaths. Then he crawls under the cover of the sleeping bag and I can only see my own.

I don't sleep.

The dreamer isn't me at all.

It's Phaedrus.

He's waking up.

A mind divided against itself ... me ... I'm the evil figure in the shadows. I'm the loathsome one ...

I always knew he would come back ...

It's a matter now of preparing for it ...

The sky under the trees looks so grey and so hopeless.

Poor Chris.

This wasn't the first time Chris had experienced his father's frailties and unstable nature. When only six years old, it seems that he and his dad had gone out on an errand. They were going to a bunk-bedders, which I presume is a place where you would buy bunks and beds. At some stage, Pirsig suffered a mental meltdown and suddenly couldn't remember what they were doing or where they were going. He had to ask Chris, who knew what they had gone out to do, but didn't know where the bunk-bedders were, and suggests they might see them if they just drive around. They did this unsuccessfully for a long time, Chris slowly coming to the realisation that his dad wasn't in control anymore. They even spent some time stopped in the middle of a road, with Pirsig not able to do anything. Cars honked and Chris had to yell at him, to snap him out of it. Pirsig didn't even know where he lived, and again he had to ask his barely school-age son. Chris knew a name, an address, but not how to get there. He told Pirsig to stop the car, and he just started asking strangers, until hours later they finally got home to a distraught and angry Mrs Pirsig.

Now here in Oregon, reflecting on these episodes, Pirsig had decided he couldn't let this happen again. He felt he should put Chris on a bus for home and check himself into a hospital in San Francisco. He felt that the trip wouldn't be wasted, and he hoped Chris would have some good memories of him as he grew up. It was quite sad, as we'd shared so much across America, and now you could sense the deterioration. We felt it as the days had got harder, and today we wouldn't even do the whole thing. We had decided to cut across from this Crater Lake/Diamond Lake area directly to Medford and on to Grants Pass. We wouldn't go all the way down to the Klamath Falls and loop around. We were getting a little fatigued and saw little value in doing so just to stick in the tyre tracks. We'd enjoy the pancakes, revel in the warming sunshine alongside a stunning lake and casually make our way down to the outside edge of the hinterland, ready for the drop down to California.

Chris found it all too much and wanted to know why they had gone to the Crater Lake. Pirsig told him it was to see the lake and Chris told him he hated it all. Pirsig was perplexed, telling him they had to keep going "until we find out what's wrong or find out why we don't know what's wrong." I do so admire Chris's stoic nature, his directness. He may weep at times, he may show his age at times, but I feel a real fondness for him. I'd probably prefer to ride across the US with him ... than his father. ZAMM gets a bit heavy here, moving away from the philosophies and back to the past, as it explains some of the posturing and political shadow-boxing and manipulations that went on within the University of Illinois leading through to Phaedrus's dismissal. This isn't a straightforward telling of course, and one that needs time to absorb it. The battles and clashes relating to the interpretation of Aristotle's teachings are central to his short-lived time teaching at the university, but that is his tale.

For us, it was another nice day, now hot, it felt good to be alive. It was Sunday, we were now encountering quite a bit of traffic as lots of people were out having a drive, just for pleasure. Quite a number of older classic vehicles were in evidence going both ways. Towards Medford, we followed a picturesque valley with the road quite close to the river. We passed a Police car going the opposite way and naturally felt guilty. I'm never sure why, but officialdom does this to most motorcyclists. We paused to admire the river and walk over a private swing bridge. We'd hardly pulled over and put the bikes on their stands when Floyd the Patrolman arrived. He'd obviously done a U turn further down the road somewhere and now was here, ready to apprehend us, I suppose. Oregon was one of the states that required motorcycles to be ridden with their headlights on during the daytime. "Oh!" we said, "we didn't know that." Rather than risk getting some sort of ticket for not having working lights, we just acquiesced and indicated that we'd be riding with them on from now on. This at least gave us a 50:50 chance of getting away. He could do another U turn and continue going the way he was going when he spotted us ... or he could now head back to where he was coming from when we first spotted him. He was a pleasant enough young man, but anyone in uniform ends up a bit institutionalised and narrow in their thinking because of the nature of their jobs. If it has a uniform, the job will have rules, and rules are things you don't interpret or think about, rules are things you follow. Rules are written down and so can be held up by the rule enforcer, who can then make utterances like "What part of this don't you understand? It says here that you must … and I must do this to you … for not doing what it says, here in the rules!" So it had seemed easier to cross our fingers and let Floyd go on his way. Disappointingly, he went our way, which left us in a bit of a quandary. Not a lot we could do about that. We waited in the sun for as long as we felt we could before heading on, deciding we'd better get some lights.

I'd been riding with my lights on all the time from the start, and first one filament went, then later the other, leaving me just the park bulb. Myles had ended up with no lights at all. Of course, Pirsig had both head and tail light bulbs on his list of spares he carried. I don't know why I didn't have a spare … it was an embarrassing oversight. Naturally, they are not something you can pick up at your local parts place. The BMW had still got a 6 volt electrical system and it was European. I was hopeful that there would be a wrecker of old VWs that might have the same bulb. As it happened we did manage to get replacements of a sort during our afternoon ride. They were sealed-beam units that didn't quite fit, so weren't ideal, but with prodigious use of duct tape, we cobbled up something. We'd followed a river road down into the sizeable town of Grants Pass. It was noticeable that we were now nearer to more civilisation, more cars, more towns, more people. We were OK with that, it just meant we had to be a lot more alert, no more somnolent respites on long straight roads, no more Fantasyland. We were focused. Pirsig called this primary America, a place of freeways and jet flights and TV and movie spectaculars. I know what he means.

Chapter *10*

THE CLIMAX

I t was near Grants Pass that Pirsig's rear chain-guard bracket fractured. It was obviously a failing of the bike model yet unusual that his bike was only 2–3 years old but with 28,000 miles beneath its wheels, whilst Myles's is 41 years old with less than 10,000 miles on the odometer. They'd both failed though. Pirsig decided not to seek a replacement, as he still intended selling the bike in a few days. He would stay in Grants Pass long enough to get it repaired. We were busy enough getting lights working. We wouldn't bother getting the chainguard repaired. The next owner might decide to source a replacement, as this one would be tricky to fix anyway. We didn't see Floyd so were quite pleased with the day. We found an adequate camp just north of Grants Pass at Indian Mary's next to a bifurcated tree and did our maintenance. It was a relaxed time. We met Yamaha-riding Don

with his lady Christy. She was a lot younger than him, and he looked like a cat with cream, almost like he couldn't believe his luck. It was as though he now had a 'trophy wife' to go with the boat, the camper and 4 x 4, the trappings of success. They were staying in the camp in a fifth-wheeler motor-home. Christy had family in the area and she was a very gregarious, enthusiastic young woman … almost flirtatious but not quite. She just wanted to talk and be part of things. She told us a limerick, she brought us beer … we liked her a lot, she was fun. They gave us a motorbike magazine. We decided we would eat out tonight. We'd have lights now, so no fear of Floyd.

We found a Chinese restaurant with a buffet to graze along. It should have been great but wasn't particularly so. The meal was good but the food very average. Kitty and I decided to go to a free outdoor concert playing on the riverside. Myles indicated that it wasn't for him and he headed back to our little tent base. The concert featured a reggae band from Hawaii who were pretty good and very popular with the young crowd. The venue was superb with grassed slopes fanning out in front of the stage. The crowd was a big mix with hippie-style groups just lapping it up. Their bare-foot, feral kids were having the time of their lives, running and jumping among the audience. They looked so happy and free, not constrained by behavioural boundaries or inhibitions. They ran and ran and ran, sibling chasing sibling. All the while the band played on, loud and proud. I sat at the back in the semi-dark observing, gently smiling as the young did what the young have always done. Kitty went up front and filmed and danced. The night was hot and sultry. The biggest audience reaction came when the band played *96 degrees in the shade* an old reggae hit from 1977. Everyone sang the chorus and swayed to the beat. Very apt, being that it had been 99 degrees when we arrived in the afternoon. It probably wasn't all that much cooler on the night. I think it did Kitty some good to absorb some youth culture from the area. She'd done quite well so far, travelling along with two old crusty curmudgeons for more than a month.

This was an awkward time for Pirsig. He knew he was deteriorating mentally. He had made plans to send Chris back to St Paul, sell the motorbike and check himself into a hospital in San Francisco. He hadn't told Chris yet. They were busy with housekeeping also. Their luggage had deteriorated a bit, and the tube of sunscreen cream had burst spreading all through the rest of their stuff. They went to the laundromat, they went to a diner and Chris read a motorcycle magazine his dad has got from a bike shop when he enquired about a new chainguard. Funny how there were so many similarities in how things unfolded for each of us. We were both in Grants Pass reading bike magazines, we both had bikes with no chainguards. The waitress in their diner showed them more attention than might have been expected. Pirsig sensed she was lonely as she came to the door to watch them ride off. The welding shop was immaculate, and the welder turned out to be a maestro. He was fussy and a little grumpy to start with, telling Pirsig that the chainguard is dirty. Pirsig did the cleaning, then was surprised that the welder didn't opt to braze the thin sheet metal material. He was very skilled and managed to weld with a suitable flame, melting the metal surfaces together almost invisibly. He asked for a dollar. Pirsig sensed he was lonely as well. He decided that he had seen loneliness everywhere he had encountered people here – the supermarket, the laundromat, the camp ground. It was all in a glance, a paradox that it was in the more crowded cities near the coast that this loneliness was apparent. Back in the areas where the people were spread thin, there hadn't been this apparent loneliness. He explains it as loneliness having nothing to do with physical distance. It is psychic distance that is critical. Back in Idaho the physical distance between people was big but the psychic distance was small. As always, Pirsig had a theory.

… people caught up in this primary America seem to go through huge portions of their lives without much consciousness of what's immediately

around them. The media have convinced them that what's right around them is unimportant. And that's why they're lonely. You see it in their faces. First the little flicker of searching, and then when they look at you, you're just a kind of object. You don't count. You're not what they're looking for. You're not on TV.

But in the secondary America we've been through, of back roads, and Chinaman's ditches, and Appaloosa horses, and sweeping mountain ranges, and meditative thoughts, and kids with pinecones and bumblebees and open sky above us mile after mile after mile, all through that, what was real, what was around us dominated. And so there wasn't much feeling of loneliness. That's the way it must have been a hundred or two hundred years ago. Hardly any people and hardly any loneliness. I'm undoubtedly overgeneralizing, but if the proper qualifications were introduced it would be true.

Technology is blamed for a lot of this loneliness, since the loneliness is certainly associated with the newer technological devices – TV, jets, freeways and so on – but I hope that it's been made plain that the real evil isn't the objects of technology but the tendency of technology to isolate people into lonely attitudes of objectivity. It's the objectivity, the dualistic ways of looking at things underlying technology, that produces the evil. That's why I went to so much trouble to show how technology could be used to destroy the evil. A person who knows how to fix motorcycles – with Quality – is less likely to run short of friends than one who doesn't. And they aren't going to see him as some sort of object either. Quality destroys objectivity every time.'

We found Grants Pass a little unusual in that, although it had close to 35,000 people living there, the library was only open on part of three days a week. Monday morning wasn't one. This was surprising, as even the small towns we'd come through had a library, some even open on Saturday ... like the one back in Bowman. They'd been stepping stones for us – they' wee where we kept in touch with the other 'real' world. It was disappointing as we'd been big fans of the service, amazed that their internet service was free and it was OK for you not to be a local card holder. Our observations were that many Americans were not great readers, the small towns often not even having a book store. Back in Mid-Ohio at the swap meet when flogging my wares, often people would buy a DVD and turn up the opportunity of the book as well, with a "I'm not much into reading." It was a TV-fed culture we were passing through. Most people recognise that libraries are important places for our communities yet often don't patronise. Never is the phrase "use it or lose it" more apt. I worked many years ago with a young Englishman who abhorred libraries, admonishing me when he would learn that was where I had been the night before. Whereas I find them serene places filled with mysterious nice-looking strangers, he found them daunting, fusty places filled with snooty rather superior sorts. I suppose it is a perception thing. Through my eyes, I deem the young women who use libraries to be far more attractive than the average, just as I have observed young women who smoke to be far less attractive than average. As they say, beauty is in the eye of the beholder, and on reflection, I recall that my workmate was a smoker so would probably have disagreed with both of my views.

Earlier in the trip a librarian, about to close up shop, helped Myles and me as we simultaneously had 'senior moments'. It is an unfortunate fact of aging that it increasingly takes longer to retrieve memories. I feel that our memories are stored in some sort of on-board library. Unfortunately, as life passing by increases the total storage of experiences, the library gets pretty full, and so the cerebral master archives a lot of stuff far away, figuratively, probably across town somewhere. The more stuff in the storage, the harder to retrieve the individual memories. Sometimes, also the microprocessor is not really up to it and takes an age to retrieve or fails to find it completely. Probably also most of us don't store our memories as well as a library does with its Dewey decimal system. In this particular instance, we'd decided something was like a scene from a Steinbeck book and told Kitty so. Upon asking more, neither of us could remember the name of the book we were each trying to remember. After spending a considerable time waiting for our mind's attendants to come back with the memories, we finally decided it wasn't going to come back, not even at 2.00am as it so often does. And so it was to a library, catching the woman with key in hand, about to shut the door. We both started describing the scenarios we had in our mind's eye. It so happened that we were both thinking of different books. I was thinking of *Tortilla Flat* whilst Myles had *Grapes of Wrath* in mind. Still a good result though. In the past, I would have just rung Mum for the answer as she was an avid, skilled crossword fan with a very good general knowledge. Disappointingly, she never left the celestial number to contact her on when she 'left the building'.

In the absence of an open library, a computer shop that also did internet hire, was found and used. The day wouldn't be a really arduous one, as this was the morning Pirsig spent getting the welding done. We finally headed away around lunchtime. It was close to 90 degrees already. The afternoon's ride was delightful to start with and could have continued to be so if we'd thought to stop and reassess the conditions. As we dropped from the hills towards the California coast, what also dropped was the temperature. A sensible person would have immediately stopped and donned more clothing. Why, after all these years, I still can't make those sensible decisions when needed to, I don't know. Initially, the ride progressed from unpleasantly hot to a perfect warm ride, moving into redwood forests for the first time. To see these enormous trees close up was a moving experience. Somehow they look like serene giants, and riding among them was wonderful. I remember feeling that we should always respect these abnormally large sequoias. They made me think of the Ents, those J R RTolkein characters who "hoom, hummed" through the forests of *The Lord of the Rings* trilogy. I idly wondered which one of these giants was Treebeard. I love also that Giant comes from Greek mythology, being one of the sons of Gaea (Earth) and Uranus (Heaven). Unfortunately, the cold began to become intrusive and spoiling. Belatedly we stopped and poured in hot coffee and found a few more warm clothes. We were now in California.

Pirsig was very reflective during this period. He was mainly recalling the finale, the time that led up to his meltdown and character removal. His battles with the Professor of Philosophy at the University of Chicago are intriguing but difficult reading. They have an intense and protracted battle over the teachings of Aristotle that is played out in the classroom where Phaedrus is taking additional classes even though he has a full-time position teaching rhetoric at Naval Pier, the University of Illinois, a rival facility. He'd already clashed with the Chairman of the Committee on Analysis of Ideas and Study of Methods who later replaces the professor for the ultimate battle with Phaedrus. Phaedrus seems to do a lot of the 'battle' winning but we know he doesn't win the 'war'. It is like a Hollywood blockbuster with good and evil fighting to the death. In this case you aren't always sure who is going to be the winner.

ZAMM and the Chautauqua and our ride were all coming to an end. The first two were moving towards a crescendo. We were just following, juggling a few of the things that must be done before we flew back to reality in less than a week's time. No one had bid on the Honda yet, and no arrangements had been made to expatriate the BMW. These quite crucial things would have to be made happen once we got to San Francisco. We all found Crescent City cold — at least for us it wasn't raining as it was in 1968. We got the makings of our evening meal and rode south, disappointed that the coast wasn't quite like our perceptions. Mistakenly, we had images of Southern California and its beaches in our minds. We'd already decided that we won't press on at the pace of the Chautauqua.

They did the ride from Grants Pass to San Francisco in two days, one being really only half a day. We would add a day to that, so there wasn't the need to push late in the day after Crescent City. In fact, while we were heading to a campsite that has been recommended … we even gave up on that. We hadn't really got enough clothing on to keep warm when riding for long periods when it was this cold.

We found a basic camp on the coast and got the tents up among a stand of spruce trees. It would have been quite idyllic if we weren't chilled to the bone. Sometimes, once your core is cold, it seems impossible to get warm again. You're cold but no one else is. This seemedto be the case here. It was around the 48 to 50-degree mark, so different from half a day ago. Another camper said how it was always like this, with the onshore cold fogs helping make the extreme temperatures further inland. He explained it all logically, but my cold, shivering body was taking up all the energy available, leaving nothing for comprehension and understanding. He also noted how much more he enjoyed these moderate temperatures when compared with the oppressive heat of the hinterland. It was hard to agree with him at the time. It was nice to walk around and explore a coastline again, our first for a long time. This was the Pacific, our Pacific, we still felt a long way from home though. We had a fire and Kitty cooked up a nice meal. Vegetarianism can be quite nice when someone with a bit of imagination is in control. My problem had always been that I don't like many vegetables, especially when they are cooked … usually overcooked. When hungry and when being polite, I can and have eaten everything put in front of me including unwashed raw potatoes, but that is another story. Where I fail, is when I have a choice. I love my meat and I love my carbohydrates. Kitty didn't think that this period had been a fair exposure to her ways, as often she had struggled to get the ingredients for nice 'cruelty-free' meals, and the bought meals during the day were at best, meat meals with the meat removed. Consequently, my pelt was showing no signs of improvement. I'd hoped that by now I would have a shiny coat and a fulsome, happy purr ... as well as being sleek and sinuous with healthy gums.

Not long into the day, we reached the famed Avenue of the Giants. Kitty and I stopped to be with the giants, to walk among them, to pay homage, to enjoy the silence. Somehow Myles, missed us stopping and for some time we were apart. This was the first time that this had happened, and of course we didn't have a plan for this eventuality. It was quite some time before we found each other again. While we wandered among the trees, waiting for him to come back, he was miles away waiting for us to come back. He thought we were ahead somewhere. It was frustrating for all of us, but on reflection, we could laugh about it. At least we did better than Rollo. He once lost a mate in Czechoslovakia for two days. The ride along the coastal route from the north of the state was quite spectacular, as sometimes we would wind in and out of little bays, nearly always kept above them by sheer bluffs and rocky outcrops. Sometimes, we would spot a private driveway leading away to a mansion in the trees or down at a tiny private beach. Now we were seeing the wealth that we knew existed in the US but hadn't seen because of the route we had taken. Whilst we would spot these appealing beaches from the bike, there was never a way down to them. The temperature had remained cool and the air damp, with the coastal fog often cutting visibility. Occasionally, we would be treated to a little warming sunshine.

Back in 1968, young Chris was all but broken, he wanted to know when they were going home. He was cold and miserable and didn't want to go on. Pirsig told him that it would be after they get to San Francisco. Chris wouldn't be swayed. Suddenly, it was like a dam bursting, his emotions and feelings cascading to the fore. He didn't want to be there, he wanted to be at home ... everything was much better, it was better when they were back in Chicago. He recalled the fun they used to have, the fun of trying to find the bunk-bed shop.

"That was fun?"

"Sure," he says, and is quiet for a long time. Then he says, "Don't you remember? You made me find all the directions home ... You used to play games with us. You used to tell us all kinds of stories and we'd go on rides to do things and now you don't do anything."

"No, you don't! You just sit and stare and you don't do anything!" I hear him crying again.

Outside the rain comes in gusts against the window, and I feel a kind of heavy pressure bear down on me. He's crying for him. It's him he misses. That's what the dream is about. In the dream...

They were unhappy, Chris was so young. He almost understood, but he was still only not quite 12. He still had the moods of his age and wasn't easily swayed. At the small settlement of Legget, they stopped at a tourist duck pond and Pirsig got some Cracker Jacks for Chris to throw to them. He could see from his demeanour, that he was still bitterly unhappy. We also paused here, riding through the tourist trap that is the famous Chandelier Tree. This is another of the gentle giants of the forest, over 300 feet high with a 21-foot diameter, it has had the indignity of having a big hole carved into it at the base for cars to drive right through. Naturally, it costs money to do this and most people stop for a photograph of the moment. I couldn't help myself but join the hundreds of thousands with a record of when they drove through a tree. A very forgettable muffin was had while we were there. It was so forgettable that I had forgotten all about it until I looked at my notes where it was recorded as 'poor' … and the beat goes on! Every time we were near the coast we went back into the freezing fogs, just as it was with them. They stopped to get out more warm clothes. While getting his gear on, Pirsig saw that Chris had gone across to a cliff edge. Pirsig recorded it dramatically.

"CHRIS!" I holler. He doesn't answer.

I go up, swiftly grab his shirt and pull him back. "Don't do that," I say.

He looks at me with a strange squint.

I get out extra clothes for him and hand them to him. He takes them but he dawdles and doesn't put them on.

There's no sense hurrying him. In this mood if he wants to wait, he can.

He waits and waits. Ten minutes, then fifteen minutes pass.

We're going to have a waiting contest.

After thirty minutes of cold winds off the ocean he asks, "Which way are we going?"

"South, now, along the coast."

"Let's go back."

"Where?"

"To where it's warmer."

That would add another hundred miles. "We have to go south now," I say.

"Why?"

"Because it would add too many miles going back."

"Let's go back."

"No. Get you warm clothes on."

He doesn't and just sits there on the ground.

After another fifteen minutes he says, "Let's go back."

"Chris, you're not running the cycle. I'm running it. We're going south."

"Why?"

"Because it's too far and because I've said so."

"Well, why don't we just go back?"

Anger reaches me. "You don't really want to know, do you?"

"I want to go back. Just tell me why we can't go back."

I'm hanging on to my temper now. "What you really want isn't to go back. What you really want is just to get me angry, Chris. If you keep it up you'll succeed!"

Flash of fear. That's what he wanted. He wants to hate me. Because I'm not him.

He looks down at the ground bitterly, and puts his warm clothes on. Then we're back on the machine and moving down the coast again.

I can imitate the father he's supposed to have, but subconsciously, at the Quality level, he sees through it and knows his real father isn't here. In all this Chautauqua talk there's been more than a touch of hypocrisy. Advice is given again and again to eliminate subject-object duality, when the biggest duality of all, the duality between me and him, remains unfaced. A mind divided against itself.

But who did it? I didn't do it. And there's no way now of undoing it...I keep wondering how far it is to the bottom of that ocean out there...

On the winding road, I had a nearly too-close encounter with a truck on a bend. I felt it wasn't going to end too badly and still maintain that I had things under control, even if I did know it was going to be a near thing. Kitty disputes this, and I am sorry to have frightened her. Motorcycling is inherently dangerous because of the lack of body protection you have. You can be in the right but still end up wearing a wooden waistcoat as Mum would have said. Myles also had an anxious moment during this part of the ride. We were cold and had been frightened so call it quits quite early. We found a KOA cabin at Manchester, a state beach park. We were still intact, which was all that mattered. The Honda had developed a bit of a misfire. After we'd established ourselves and warmed up, Kitty and I decided we'd go out for a bought meal in nearby Point Arena. Myles settled for another afternoon of tinkering with his little baby, trying to find why it was not running on both cylinders properly.

In contrast to the Pirsigs' precarious relationship at this point in time, Kitty and I had a lovely time. Point Arena was an old hippie, arty-crafty little town of only a few hundred with a library for emails and a wonderful café that doubled as an organic food co-op. It had a good selection of suitable vegetarian meals for us. I felt finally like I had been welcomed into some sort of inner sanctum. This was the first time whilst eating out that I had been acknowledged as 'normal', even though I didn't think we were 'alternative' enough … just by being vegetarian. It was a start. I think the old motorbike outside gave us a bit of street cred though. This was Mendocino County, and it felt good. This wee town had a wide sloping main street and a very relaxed friendly aura. It didn't have the overt patriotism that we had experienced earlier in the trip. I don't think we saw a star-spangled banner anywhere. Possibly that helped us feel more at home. We were eager to tell Myles of this little gem and were a little sorry he has missed out on it. We returned to the camp to find he has been quite happy getting his fingers dirty and slowly imbibing a bottle of syrah wine, not in the least bit envious of our outing. We did our laundry and finished off the wine, thankful for the dregs. We were only a day from San Francisco.

The ZAMM riders were still fighting bitterly. It was still a battle of wills. Pirsig admitted he felt as though he was living life as a sham, always trying to please others. When this time he had stood up to Chris, he was hurt because he recognised that Chris was just sticking to his beliefs. They were at that precarious point of an irrevocable split. Pirsig stopped because he was tired, and again Chris rounded on him, wanting to know why they weren't pressing on. Pirsig told him to run around in circles while he rested, and I can imagine that going down like a lead balloon. I think Pirsig was at the end of his tether and unable to manage his young offspring as a father should. They rode on, and he came to the realisation that Chris was like Phaedrus, the old Pirsig. It all seemed to fit in his thoughts ... getting into trouble, being driven by forces he was not really aware of. They stopped for something to eat, but again Chris refused and went back to his old sore stomach routine ... just like earlier in the trip – the same sore stomach that had never been able to be cured or even confirmed by the doctors as being real. They were both almost at the point of breakdown. There were fewer than 10 pages to go, and there is a sense of impending doom. A happy ending was not in sight.

I look up and see that Chris is crying.

"Now what?" I say.

"My stomach. It's hurting,"

"Is that all?"

"No. I just hate everything ... I'm sorry I came ... I hate this trip ... I thought this was going to be fun, and it isn't any fun ... I'm sorry I came." He is a truth-teller, like Phaedrus. And like Phaedrus he looks at me now with more and more hatred. The time has come.

"I've been thinking, Chris, of putting you on the bus here with a ticket for home."

His face has no expression on it, then surprise mixed with dismay.

I add. "I'll go on myself with the motorcycle and see you in a week or two. There's no sense forcing you to continue on a vacation you hate."

Now it's my turn to be surprised. His expression isn't relieved at all. The dismay gets worse and he looks down and says nothing.

He seems caught off balance now, and frightened.

He looks up. "Where would I stay?"

"Well you can't stay at our house now, because other people are there. You

can stay with grandma and grandpa."

"I don't want to stay with them."

"You can stay with your aunt."

"She doesn't like me. I don't like her."

"You can stay with your other grandma and grandpa."

"I don't want to stay there either."

I name some others but he shakes his head.

"Well, who then?"

"I don't know."

"Chris, I think you can see for yourself what the problem is. You don't want to be on this trip. You hate it. Yet you don't want to stay with anyone or go anywhere else. All these people I've mentioned you either don't like or they don't like you."

He's silent but tears now form.

A woman at another table is looking at me angrily. She opens her mouth as though to say something. I turn a heavy gaze on her for a long time until she closes her mouth and goes back to eating.

Now Chris is crying hard and others look over from the other tables.

"Let's go for a walk, "I say, and get up without waiting for the check.

At the cash register the waitress says, "I'm sorry the boy isn't feeling good."

I nod, pay, and we're outside.

I look for a bench somewhere in the luminous haze but there is none. Instead we climb on the cycle and go slowly south looking for a restful place to pull off.

I wanted to scream at Pirsig that he was doing it all wrong, couldn't he just weather the storm? Couldn't he just understand what the enormity of sending him home on a bus alone would be like? The kid wasn't even 12, you pillock! It didn't get any better, as a short while later he found somewhere to stop.

I look at Chris and see a puzzled, empty look in his eyes, but as soon as I ask him to sit down, some of the anger and hatred of this morning reappear.

"Why?" he asks.

"I think it's time we should talk."

"Well, talk," he says. All the old belligerence is back. It's the 'kind father' image he can't stand. He knows the 'niceness' is false.

"What about the future?" I say. Stupid thing to ask.

"What about it?" he says.

"I was going to ask what you planned to do about the future."

"I'm going to let it be." Contempt shows now.

The fog opens for a moment, revealing the cliff we are on, then closes again, and a sense of inevitability about what is happening comes over me. I'm being pushed toward something and the objects in the corner of the eye and the objects in the center of the vision are all of equal intensity now, all together in one, and I say, "Chris, I think it is time to talk about some things you don't know about."

He listens a little. He senses something is coming.

"Chris, you're looking at a father who was insane for a long time, and is very close to it again."

And not just close anymore. It's here. The bottom of the ocean.

"I'm sending you home not because I'm angry with you but because I'm afraid of what can happen if I continue to take responsibility for you."

And his face doesn't show any change of expression. He doesn't understand yet what I am saying.

"So this is going to be good-bye, Chris and I'm not sure we'll see each other anymore."

This is cruel brutal stuff and not what you want to read after struggling through 400 pages, it is a family show after all. This is why Myles thought Pirsg was bit of a hard bastard. I give him the benefit of the doubt, because I know he is suffering from a mental illness or disorder. There was some pretty graphic stuff as Pirsig told Chris further that 'they' had been saying the same sorts of things about him, that his troubles were in his head and Chris sank to the ground wailing and rocking. Pirsig could hear a truck coming through the fog. His urgency in raising Chris was strident and heartfelt. He wanted to run for the cliff but fought the urge, knowing he had to get Chris up and on a bus ... then the cliff would be OK. Chris sat up, staring and crying, the truck stopped safely and asked if they needed a lift. It was waved on and they were alone again.

Just like our journey, there was a fascination, yet also a fear of ending the book. Because of the uncertainty of the way it was unfolding, it was easy to take a break and take a few deep breaths. You wanted to find out what happened next ... but there was also a sense of dread, because you didn't know if you'd like the ending. I was like this even though I had read the book before. For us, there is no rushing to cliff edges, other than to look over and photograph. We rode off in the cold morning air, buoyed by the fact that this was the last day riding, and we'd made contact with Dave and Carol in Redwood City just out of San Francisco. That is where we would stay for our last few days, facilitating our withdrawal from the US. The road was tightly twisting and undulating. It would be immense fun if we weren't always just a little too cold for comfort. We really needed our winter riding clothing for this part of the ride. We passed by a sign noting that this part of the roadside was maintained and kept clean by the local Norton Owners Club. This was quite a change from the usual church and general do-gooding groups that usually were the ones who do this. I reflected that one of the bonuses of travelling across the US in comparison to almost everywhere else I have ridden is that it was so clean. There is a great civic pride in the towns and the sides of the highways never show signs of litter etc. What they haven't got a hold of yet is the idea that there is such a thing as 'visual pollution'. This concept is completely alien to them, and gaudy edifices and signs often dominate what could be an

exquisite vista. Yet again in Pat's words, "It's the American way!" The glitz and glamour of advertising has a lot to answer for.

We stopped for fuel at a tiny station with a couple of pumps and the payment was made across the road at the Ocean Cove Grocery, a minuscule old shop which was part of a historic house with wooden shingles on the walls. The stone walls lining the road and tight corner where this was looks like it should be in the UK, not the US. The female attendant asked us which way we were going, and on learning that we were heading for State Highway 101, she told us we would hit the sunshine in 20 miles. We noted later that she was spot on. The cold fog banks just hovered over the actual coastal strip and burned off a little further inland. This was a lovely looking, little twisty spot that we rode again so Kitty could film us. It was no hardship at all, and if Groundhog Day struck right now … it wouldn't be all bad. Once we headed inland, we did hit the sunshine and immediately warmed up. The cold had been the penalty of

following Pirsig's ride. As it happens, I think I was too coast-focused and not vigilant enough, as I think they left the coast one road before us. We had a stop in Guerneville where Myles found a mower shop that just also happened to be a treasure trove of old British bikes. The owner had an old BSA Gold Star racer lined up next to a couple of World War Two side-valve BSAs and a couple of Triumphs. This was our kind of shop. Myles was given a second-hand coil and high-tension lead, which may or may not fix the intermittent misfire. We were now on the home run and spirits of course were high. Without even having been there, I knew there was a magic about San Francisco, something special. Perhaps it is the fact that it is a harbour city like our Wellington, perhaps it is the iconic bridges, maybe it is because of all the exposure it has had through movies and TV over the years. It could be Steve McQueen's *Bullitt* or it could be the Scott McKenzie song San Francisco – be sure to wear some flowers in your hair from the summer of love (1967) when 100,000 young people flocked to and made famous Haight-Ashbury. We all had our own images of San Francisco and carried them with us in eager anticipation.

But the final climax of ZAMM was unfolding just up the coast. Chris had been crying and finally came out with:

"Why did you leave us?"

When?

"At the hospital!"

There was no choice. The police prevented it.

"Wouldn't they let you out?"

No.

"Well then, why couldn't you open the door?"

What door?

"The glass door!"

A kind of slow electric shock passes through me. What glass door is he talking about?

"Don't you remember?" he says. "We were standing on one side and you were on the other side and Mom was crying."

I've never told him about that dream. How could he know about that? Oh, no.

We're in another dream. That's why my voice sounds so strange.

I couldn't open that door. They told me not to open it. I had to do everything they said.

"I thought you didn't want to see us," Chris says. He looks down.

The look of terror in his eyes all these years.

Now I see the door. It is in a hospital.

This is the last time I will see them. I am Phaedrus, that is who I am, and they are going to destroy me for speaking the Truth.

It has all come together.

Chris cries softly now. Cries and cries and cries. The wind from the ocean blows through the tall stems of grass all around us and the fog begins to lift.

"Don't cry, Chris. Crying is just for children."

After a long time, I give him a rag to wipe his face with. We gather up our stuff and pack it on the motorcycle. Now the fog suddenly lifts and I see the sun on his face makes his expression open in a way I've never seen it before. He puts on his helmet, tightens the strap, then looks up.

"Were you really insane?"

Why should he ask that?

No!

Astonishment hits. But Chris's eyes sparkle.

"I knew it," he says.

Then he climbs on the cycle and we are off.

Chris kept repeating how he knew it … he knew it all along. He knew his dada wasn't gaga, not really insane like they'd said. They'd gone inland and, like us, were warmed by the sun, relieved to be out of the bone-chilling cold fogs. They found a picnic spot, and Pirsig told Chris that he was sleepy and going to take a nap. Inclusively, Chris says he would too. As a father, I can identify with these little treasured, shared times, both finally going the same direction, at the same speed. When they awoke it was so hot that Pirsig decided to ride helmetless, as it as allowed in California. He hooked his helmet to the bars. Chris wanted to follow his dad's example, and initially Pirsig told him he needed it for safety but recanted when Chris retorts that he wasn't wearing his. They rode together helmetless, laughing after the first vocal interchange when they learned there was no need to shout, now they didn't have helmets on. Chris was now happy and calling out how great things were, and Pirsig felt him hold onto his shoulders and stand up on the foot pegs. Suddenly, and this was the one big strong image I had taken from the book when I first read it in 1977, suddenly Chris can see. He can see it *all* now – he can see what his father is seeing. He is looking over the top of the shoulder, instead of looking straight into his father's back ... or out the side to a blurring view. This vision takes him into his father's world. He is now riding through the countryside, enjoying it, revelling in it, he can see it as it approaches. No longer is he just sitting there enduring this almost endless road trip.

I think you must forgive Pirsig, simply because of the warm way he captures this familial revival.

"What do you see?" I ask.

"It's all different."

We head into a grove again, and he says, "Don't you get scared?"

"No, you get used to it."

After a while he says, "Can I have a motorcycle when I get old enough?"

"If you take care of it."

"What do you have to do?"

"Lots of things. You've been watching me."

"Will you show me all of them?"

"Sure."

"Is it hard?"

"Not if you have the right attitudes. It's having the right attitudes that's hard."

"Oh."

After a while I see he is sitting down again. Then he says, "Dad?"

"What?"

"Will I have the right attitudes?"

"I think so," I say. "I don't think that will be any problem at all."

And so we ride on and on, down through Ukiah, and Hopland, and Cloverdale, down into the wine country. The freeway miles seem so easy now. The engine which has carried us halfway across a continent drones on and on in its continuing oblivion to everything but its own internal forces. We pass through Asti and Santa Rosa, and Petaluma and Novato, on the freeway that grows wider and fuller now, swelling with cars and trucks and buses full of people, and soon by the road are houses and boats and the water of the Bay.

Trials never end, of course. Unhappiness and misfortune are bound to occur as long as people live, but there is feeling now, that was not here before, and is not just on the surface of things, but penetrates all the way through: We've won it. It's going to get better now. You can sort of tell these things.

And so finally, with a happy ending to ZAMM, we also rode into San Francisco in a happy mood. We first glimpsed the Golden Gate bridge from a distance, poking out of the top of a low candy-floss fog. Later as we rode across this man-made wonder, I chuckled recalling Myles's words from way back in Canada about the North Americans "doing good bridges". Talk about an understatement. For me it was a wonderful thrill, the BMW was

purring contentedly, as they do. With their characteristic flat, rounded but muted burble, it really is like a cat's purr, one where the cat never pauses for breath. Behind me, Myles was struggling, the Honda needed that coil but although the bike stuttered and hiccuped giving Myles an uncertain ride, they remained in my mirrors all the way. With the GPS activated, Kitty unerringly navigated us to the Zen Center. Here, we were greeted with respect and warmth. We arrived unannounced and were shown the nicest of hospitality. They made us a cup of tea and invited us to stay as long as we liked. We were not the first to visit, but they made us welcome as though we were. Of course, the sad postscript to ZAMM is that, ten years after the ride, Chris was living and studying here … and was killed a couple of streets over in a botched robbery. The Center has his ashes. It is a very calm and peaceful place, I'm sure he rests well.

It was Wednesday, late afternoon. The *Zen* ride was over … the story finished, the rest was irrelevant. Sunday, Myles and I would fly home, Monday Kitty would leave for Seattle. The Honda would be bought on the eBay auction with the sole bid at 2 minutes to go on Saturday, picked up on Sunday morning … good result. Our hosts Dave and Carol and their friends excelled themselves, providing a welcoming base for those few days. It was a blur. We rode out to Alice's Restaurant *in* the hills, visited Haight-Ashbury, rode cable cars and trains, gave to beggars, saw Fisherman's Wharf and arranged the shipping of the BMW.

ZEN AND THE LAST HURRAH

252

Chapter Eleven

FINAL REFLECTIONS

For many, a road trip is a rite of passage ... often a signal of their attainment of adulthood. It shows to all that the apron strings have been cut. Some will only have that one significant journey of this ilk in their life and hold those memories dear forever. For others, they need the stimulus on a regular basis, to reinvigorate them as much mentally as physically. It may appear to be overstating it, but when on the road you are back in a hunter-gatherer mode. Each day begins with you not knowing what will be around each new corner, not knowing where you will eat, sleep or even go to the toilet. There is no déjà vu on the road. Normally, our lives have these little things repeated in a comfortable pattern. Take away that pattern, and for many, it is replaced by fear. I must confess to a momentary feeling of trepidation when contemplating this journey. I knew that we'd be camping out, and the uncertainty flashed up the possibility of a random attack, of being robbed ... of being a victim of some act of asinine stupidity that would be whistled across the globe on the world's news wires. Fortunately, these thoughts were just triggered by the unknown and soon passed. "Never worry about things that might not happen," Kitty once told me.

We saw back-roads America, the America I knew we'd like. It was nothing like television, and we take that as a highlight … a bonus of the trip. This was not America that most tourists bother with. Apart from Niagara Falls and a small part of Yellowstone Park, we didn't do the mainstream or popular thing … maybe that will be next time, but probably not. It was also hard to comprehend that what we had passed through was a sample of the world's most powerful nation after 10 years of economic boom. Again we liked that, it made everything far more easy to relate to, far more humble and enjoyable. Our senses were not often assaulted by the 'frenzy of consumerism' that usually typifies the United States … and we find alienating. Pirsig had chosen his route well. Ask us, "Did you enjoy America?", and the answer is a resounding "Yes!" from all of us.

We may share a language and historical background (mainly), and yet most mundane day-to-day things were different and that always helps sustain interest … and gives peripheral enjoyment. Those differences always give rise to the inconsequential questions like, "Why does America have red lenses for their car and motorbike blinkers … while the rest of the world has amber ones?" The rules of the road have not been able to be fully explained to us by any of the people we've met and thought to ask, "Who goes first when all four traffic lights are flashing?" "You give way to your left, but I think you just take turns at going through … and don't go fast!" No one seems to know the minutiae or official protocols, and it doesn't appear to matter much.

We'd started with *The Last Hurrah* as our primary focus, but fortuitously allowed ZAMM to take over when *The Last Hurrah* was looking like a bit of a fizzer. I feel that this gave our ride its quality. We don't fuss whether that is with a big Q or not. It provided the most wonderful of routes and always gave us something to relate to. The battered little book we carried was almost like a talisman. Maybe it did have magic powers … after all, it did tell us where to go, and what to do. It may not have changed my life, as others have claimed, but it certainly has provided a wonderful mid-life interlude. I am not sure if the constant and detailed analysis of thoughts, deeds and machinery benefited us, but they have been of interest, even though I prefer to learn real things … non-challenging things. I'd quite like to know how Amazonian Indians cut their toe-nails?

The countryside was vast and varied … and almost never like New Zealand. The roadkill was even new for us, with prairie dogs and gophers and things we couldn't identify. The food was often terrible, my companions never. I think the most critical decision when it comes to travelling enjoyment is your choice of fellow travellers and I struck the jackpot again. I thank them for the memories they've left me with. Almost finally, the bikes … magnificent. Over 40 years old and they gave better than sterling service. I salute their makers.

And finally, finally, to Robert Pirsig and the rest of the ZAMM crew … their Chautauqua went down in history, a sometimes wild ride, a ride of discovery on a personal and spiritual level. You led and we followed. I thank you for the experiences, and I thank you for the thoughts. Those challenging thoughts may have been a bit deep for us at times, but they've made us think and reflect. We've completed what is probably the only 'almost' re-enactment of the original journey. We're proud of that. There have been many Pirsig Pilgrims and pilgrimages, but we'll always feel that we did it the right way – the only way that could fully capture the spirit of the Chautauqua. There could never be the 'feel' of the journey on anything other than those two motorbikes. An air-conditioned motor-home or 1300 cc Harley Davidson is not ever going to give the same feedback as the little 305 cc Honda Superhawk. It would never even be close to being the same journey. The hills and headwinds would never be the same … the level of discomfort would be different, only the vistas would be constant – and they can be bought on a postcard.

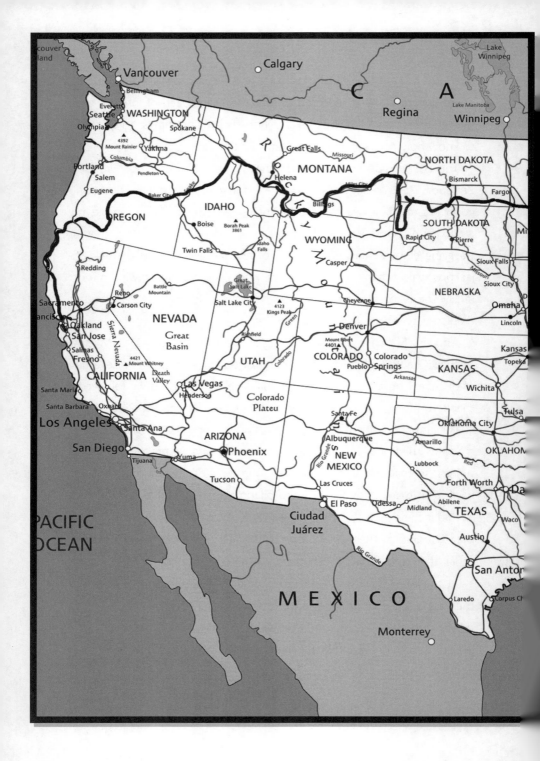

ZEN AND THE LAST HURRAH

256

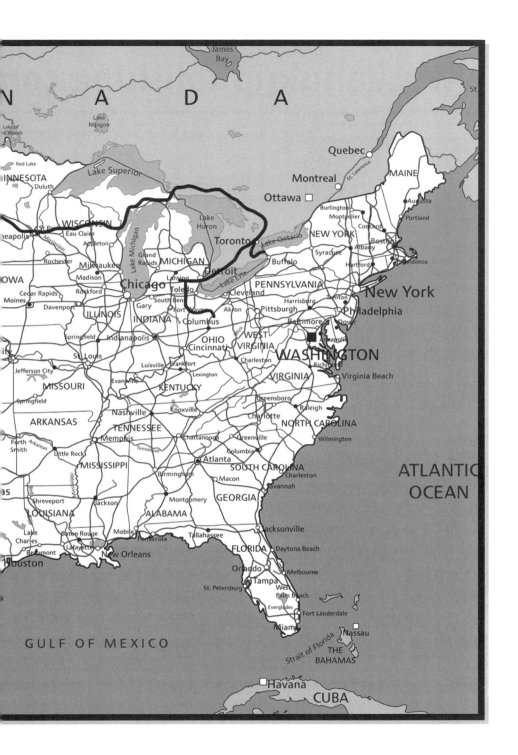

FINAL REFLECTIONS
257

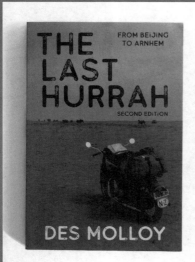